Leveling the Playing Field—Part I

▽

What You Need to Know to Develop a Financial Game Plan

William E Hauenstein, MBA, CRPC

iUniverse, Inc.
Bloomington

Leveling the Playing Field—Part I
What You Need to Know to Develop a Financial Game Plan

The information, ideas, and suggestions in this book are not intended to render professional advice. Before following any suggestions contained in this book, you should consult your personal accountant or other financial advisor. Neither the author nor the publisher shall be liable or responsible for any loss or damage allegedly arising as a consequence of your use or application of any information or suggestions in this book.

Risk Tolerance Questionnaire (Appendix D) is the property of FinaMetrica Pty Limited. Used by permission.

iUniverse books may be ordered through booksellers or by contacting:

iUniverse
1663 Liberty Drive
Bloomington, IN 47403
www.iuniverse.com
1-800-Authors (1-800-288-4677)

Because of the dynamic nature of the Internet, any Web addresses or links contained in this book may have changed since publication and may no longer be valid. The views expressed in this work are solely those of the author and do not necessarily reflect the views of the publisher, and the publisher hereby disclaims any responsibility for them.

Any people depicted in stock imagery provided by Thinkstock are models, and such images are being used for illustrative purposes only.

Certain stock imagery © Thinkstock.

ISBN: 978-1-4759-3471-7 (sc)
ISBN: 978-1-4759-3472-4 (hc)
ISBN: 978-1-4759-3473-1 (e)

Library of Congress Control Number: 2012912178

Printed in the United States of America

iUniverse rev. date: 8/2/2012

Contents

Preface

In my twenty-three years of helping families with their finances, I have learned that most do not have a budget or even a last will and testament, and as a result, the median financial picture is not very pretty. In a recent study by the Kaiser Family Foundation as reported in the June 2011 AARP Bulletin, the median Medicare recipient has $2,000 in retirement savings. This is not a typo.

Members of the baby-boom generation were taught to believe that Social Security and Medicare, which they paid for with deductions from their paychecks their entire lives, would always be there for them. Other "progressive" social programs such as food stamps, unemployment insurance, the earned income tax credit, low income housing, welfare, and Medicaid were created to temporarily help those in need. Unfortunately, many welcomed these programs as a permanent part of their financial plan. As a result, dependence upon these US government-sponsored programs are at an all-time high and will continue to rise in the years ahead unless Americans begin a personal austerity plan combining debt reduction with prudent long-term investment and risk transfer plans.

Now, with costs of these programs increasing greater than our ability to fund them through economic growth, taxes will have to increase and/or services be reduced. Will Americans be ready for such an eventuality?

A combination of Yogi Berra tongue-in-cheek quotes makes a lot of sense: "You can observe a lot by watching," and "If you don't know where you are going, you'll wind up somewhere else." Unfortunately, most American families end up somewhere financially they did not want to be. As I will explain in this book, a sound financial footing is essential for creating and maintaining wealth. Beginning at an early age, armed with sound financial principles, commitment to your goals, and responding effectively to the challenges life will place in your path is your best "methodology to prosperity." Try to plan as best you can, and if you need help (which most everyone does), by all means, work with qualified, experienced advisers. Do not let your finances become an anxiety magnet, leading to family arguments, misallocated resources, and ultimately fewer achieved personal, professional, and financial goals.

Since I cannot personally provide service to everyone who may benefit from the words of this book, my goal is to help as many readers reduce the financial stress in their lives by helping them understand how their personal experiences help shape their decision-making process and help them develop a knowledge base vital for development and implementation of a sound, holistic financial plan.

Each one should use whatever gift he has received to serve others, faithfully administering God's grace in its various forms.
(1 Peter 4:10, New International Version).

About the Author

William E Hauenstein was born into a US military family and was taught the basics of financial planning by his father, Tsgt. Wendell Hauenstein, beginning at age seven. After serving in the United States Air Force for twenty-one years, Wendell decided to retire and work as a law enforcement official in Biloxi, Mississippi, but during his retirement physical at the Keesler Air Force Base Hospital, he was diagnosed with extremely elevated blood pressure and was immediately placed in the Coronary Intensive Care Unit. That evening, Wendell suffered three massive heart attacks and was revived each time, with his guardian angel lending a helping hand. Unable to work, he accepted medical retirement and relocated the family to Albuquerque, New Mexico.

Every few weeks at the kitchen table, Wendell would teach William the basics of cash flow planning (using matchsticks where one match equaled ten dollars), how to write a check, what an emergency fund was, how you need to prepare for the unexpected, what entitlement plans were, and who to contact at the military base in case of emergencies. Pretty heavy stuff for such a young child, but Wendell believed William had the skills and maturity to handle the family finances.

Being a career military man, Wendell was organized and punctual and created his budgetary system using one four-by-six-inch note card, along the top indicating months, listing bills to be paid, in alphabetical order, of course, down the left side. He then drew a diagonal line in each box with the date the bill should arrive on the top left and the date he mailed the payment on the bottom right of the box. Since money was tight, he did not use credit cards and did not believe in impulse buying (even though his children tried to convince him otherwise). After a few months, William became proficient at understanding his system and what needed to be done. William was well aware of the family's finances and took odd jobs, such as selling newspapers on the corner, shoveling snow in the winter, and mowing lawns whenever possible to help make ends meet.

Understanding that finances were important to long-term family stability, William focused his energy on being a good student. Pragmatic by nature, he earned a Bachelor of Science degree in computer science and an MBA from the University of New Mexico and worked as a contract employee for Sandia National Laboratories in Albuquerque, New Mexico, and later as a systems analyst for McDonnell Douglas Corporation in Long Beach, California. Working as an information technology specialist was satisfying, but when corporate politics became more important than doing what he believed was right, he left that profession and thought about what he wanted his legacy to be. *"When you swish your hand in a bucket of water and then take it out, there were a few waves when you were doing it, but soon the water becomes still as though nothing had happened."* William said. *"I wanted to make a difference that stood the test of time and going back to my roots, I felt that helping families with their finances would provide the parents and grandparents the opportunity to spend more time with their family and give them the opportunity to build their own legacies."*

Sometimes things happen for a reason and provide a path for us to take.

Professional Qualifications

Education:

University of New Mexico

- Bachelor of Science, computer science, 1984
- MBA, management science, 1986

College for Financial Planning

- Chartered Retirement Planning Counselor, 2007

Professional Designations

- Series 4—Registered Options Principal Exam, 2005
- Series 6—Investment Company and Variable Contracts Exam, 1988
- Series 7—General Securities Representative Exam, 1993
- Series 24—General Securities Principal Exam, 1999
- Series 63—Uniform Securities Agent State Law Exam, 1988
- Series 65—Uniform Registered Investment Adviser Law Exam, 1996
- Life, Disability & Variable Insurance—Insurance Exam—1993

Disciplinary Information

I have no material disciplinary events to report.

Introduction

When you think about the financial markets, what emotions do you feel? Fear? Distrust? Anger? Greed? Apathy? Disillusionment? Excitement?

Who do you think is in control of the markets? "Big Banks"? Hedge funds? Governments?

How do you feel about your personal financial situation? Improving? Trying to keep your head above water? Frustrated?

How do you feel about the US national debt? About the pension plans that are underfunded? About the crumbling national infrastructure? About the cost of medical care? The cost of education? The unemployment rate?

Do you think the federal government is working on your behalf? On behalf of lobbyists? Large contributors? Anyone who will help them get reelected?

How do you make sense of all of the above?

All are good questions, and all are debatable. One thing is certain, however, and that is uncertainty. Nowhere in the US Constitution or Declaration of Independence does it say that anyone is entitled to certainty in anything. We must deal with things as they come and be as prepared as we can for all the uncertainty life throws at us.

This book is intended to help deliver certainty, but only after you work hard at preparation, planning, and practice.

CHAPTER ONE

▽

Preparation

Someone is sitting in the shade today because
someone planted a tree a long time ago.
—Warren Buffet

Success, however you define it, doesn't just fall into your lap; it is earned over an extended period of time.

Section One—Factors to Consider

Prepare to succeed. We have all heard the clichés about how practice and preparation are essential for success, and we all know that the more effort one puts into preparation, the more likely success will follow. The difficult thing to figure out is this: "What do I practice and how do I prepare?" The answer depends upon many factors, including time, knowledge, ability to trust, understanding, and innate ability. Let's discuss each of these factors.

Time

First, and foremost, is time. The clock never stops, and neither do the demands placed upon us. Everyone has the same 168 hours per week. What we choose to do with those hours is, hopefully,

1

more controlled by our choices and desires than by necessity or the demands of others.

According to the 2010 American Time Use Survey (US Department of Labor, Bureau of Labor Statistics, 2011), an average American's day is composed of sleeping for eight hours and twenty-three minutes; performing work and work-related activities for four hours and twenty-four minutes; watching television for two hours and thirty-one minutes; leisure and sporting activities two hours and nine minutes; household chores for one hour and forty-one minutes; eating, drinking, and personal care for two hours and one minute; leaving two hours and fifty-one minutes for everything else, such as education, shopping, caring for household members, telephone calls, e-mail, social networking, and religious activities.

Since this is an average, your day is probably much different, and you are wondering how you accomplish so many things in such a short period of time. Many of us forego sleep to work extra hours or take the children to their soccer games, while others are retired and spend more time volunteering or babysitting the grandchildren. Since time is the one thing none of us can manufacture, it is our most valuable commodity.

The point I am trying to make is that time is valuable and you need to invest it wisely, or many of the things you want to accomplish in life will be left for someone else. Today is the beginning of the rest of your life. Treat it that way and you can accomplish anything you set your mind to.

Please see Appendix B for a Time Budget Worksheet. Its goal is to help you understand which tasks you spend your time doing and then manage your time effectively so you can accomplish those things that are most important to you and your family.

Knowledge

You've probably heard the expression "knowledge is power," but what does that mean to you? For many, knowledge, when combined with personal experience, provides them with the basis to confidently make prudent decisions.

For example, if you know a stove is hot, you won't touch it with your bare hands. Alternatively, if you do not know whether the stove is hot or cold, will you assume it is cold and lay your hands upon it? Probably not, because you may have been burned by a hot object before, remember the pain, and approach the stove with caution (better safe than sorry).

Okay, now let us assume that you will receive an extra $500 per month of income from writing a jingle used on a television commercial as long as it is deemed beneficial in the company's advertising strategy. So what do you do with that extra money? Since the income is not guaranteed, you should not increase your fixed expenses by that amount; instead, you should treat it as a windfall and use it to your best advantage. "What could that be?" you ask. You might add it to your children's college fund, your retirement plan, or to the savings for that family vacation you have always dreamed of.

More complex items can be broken down into parts to determine how each part may affect the overall choice. In other words, one should consider the many inputs when analyzing a complex situation. One example is relocating your family to another state or country for work. Factors to consider are not just quantitative but also qualitative. Quantitative factors can be compiled with a calculator or spreadsheet, while the qualitative factors must be given a quantifiable number to add to the formula. Quantitative factors include such things as income, benefits, cost of living, etc. Qualitative factors include quality and availability of education, how much more or less you like your new job, climate, social events, proximity of friends and family, and cultural activities.

You should also weight each factor based upon its importance to your situation. Yes, this is an analytical approach and may not appeal to everyone, but you can see how thinking through the process can help you make a more informed decision.

For many, the development of a detailed financial plan will turn information into knowledge, thus providing the roadmap to follow.

Ability to Trust

Many of you will recall that when Ronald Reagan uttered the phrase "Trust, but verify" at the signing of the Intermediate-Range Nuclear Forces (INF) Treaty with Russia in 1987, most everyone in the audience was laughing. Just as the Seinfeld show was a series of episodes about "nothing," President Reagan's maxim evoked a laugh because it is true.

With the uncertainty that prevails in today's economic, social, and political realms, with the media blasting stories that cause us to wonder if our best times are behind us, no wonder many investors have given up and become savers, trying to preserve what wealth they have. Here is a quote that summarizes this mind-set very well:

> The average American family has lost 9 percent of their household net worth in just the last three months of 2008—the fastest disintegration of wealth in more than seven decades. In fact, the majority of families were reporting a drop of 25 percent in their household worth in the past year alone. Pretty pessimistic stuff ... our national confidence is in pieces, our personal expectations shattered. *Trust has collapsed.* We have little tolerance now for promises and pledges. We don't trust anyone anymore. (Luntz, 2009)

So, with that as our backdrop, how do you know when it is okay to trust what someone has told you? After independent verification, of course. The thing about human beings is that we are human, able to make judgments, opinions, statements, even without knowing both sides of the argument. The search for truth is elusive but should be on everyone's agenda when you make a decision that can affect not only yourself but many others. As my father told me many years ago, "You have been given the ability to make up your own mind, but doing so without independent research is merely espousing someone else's opinion."

Here is an excerpt of a newsletter article I wrote in early 2011:

> One big problem now is uncertainty. With the earth shifting beneath our feet because of government intervention (regulations, incentive programs, monetary policy, changes in accounting standards, etc.), no wonder businesses are reluctant to invest for their future as the game may change. I have always said that if you change the rules of the game, you change the game. It is difficult to predict the outcome of change and its overall impact on various industries. This "collateral damage" should be quantified as much as possible and not create a systemic breakdown of our financial system.
>
> So, with all the recent changes, how's that working out for you? Is your portfolio performing to your expectations? If you are lucky enough to be the recipient of a pension, is it safe? Are you enjoying the volatility? Well, it seems the only time when markets are not volatile is when they are closed. Headline risk, fast trading, and lower volume are all reasons for higher than normal volatility. The market

is trading on rumors, and that is not a good thing. Don't get caught up in that. Sometimes it is better to be out of the market or have downside protection strategies in place to preserve your wealth. *I believe most would choose to not be poor than to be rich, and I am not just speaking about money.*

Understanding

Understanding is the essential component that turns information into knowledge and ultimately into wisdom. In math, one must understand the concept of the operation you are trying to solve. There are infinite possibilities for addition, so it is impossible to memorize each potential equation. If you understand the basics of addition (e.g., 1+1=2 or 2+4=6), you can solve any addition problem placed in front of you. Some will say, "I will just take out my calculator or smartphone and I do not even have to understand why; it will give me the correct answer." This is true of simple, impersonal subjects, but there is no calculator or smartphone for determining which condiment tastes better on a hamburger, be it ketchup, mustard, mayonnaise, or some combination. You must learn these things for yourself through trial and error.

Small purchases or commitments do not demand painstaking research, but creating and implementing financial, investment, and legacy plans should. For example, most investors are trying to maximize the value of their account with the minimum risk. Sound familiar? There are many risks to consider, and each are important, some more and some less at different points during your lifetime. For those beginning the planning process, it is important to know the basic components of the type of financial plan you are working on, gain an understanding as to what the inputs to those components of your plan mean, and understand how they may affect your overall situation now and in the future.

Innate Ability

The Constitution of the United States of America states clearly, "All men are created equal and are endowed by their creator with unalienable rights that among these are life, liberty, and the pursuit of happiness." It does not say that we all have the same abilities or that one life is worth more than any other.

As a youngster, my life's ambition was to become a professional basketball player. I would spend time watching Oscar Robertson, nicknamed the "Big O" (O as in Oscar, not a zero!), on our family's black-and-white television (we couldn't afford a color TV) and try to emulate his command of the game. I practiced at the local park or public school even when no one was around and thought about winning the game on a last-second shot or making a steal to prevent the other team from having a chance to win. My plan was on track until about the seventh grade when I reached my current height of five feet, eight inches tall! The dream of playing the "four" (power forward) position (or any position for that matter) in the NBA was just that—a dream—and a few years later a fond memory.

At that point in my life, I never imagined being a financial adviser and author, and little did I know I was blessed with the ability to understand complex financial markets and to help families with their finances. After writing many articles for clients over the years, this is my first book, and I hope it will help you become a better steward of your finances. You might even learn a little about yourself, your current financial adviser, and your family in the process.

What abilities have you been blessed with? Knowing your strengths and weaknesses is important so you can be successful at your chosen profession. As my wife says, if you do what you love, you never work a day in your life. I thank her for believing in me and for providing encouragement and support all these years.

So when you are embarking on the path of making decisions

that will impact the outcome of not only your future but those of your family and close friends, carefully think through the factors. After doing so, you will be more confident and have the will to act.

Section Two—Mental: Can You Do It Yourself?

Of course you can. The real question is, can someone else help you which results in an even better outcome (*or for those who wish to retire someday, should I say an even better future income*)? If you are a specialist in behavioral finance, investments, insurance, taxes, and estate planning, then, you can truly "do it yourself," assuming you have the time. Otherwise, it is probably better to assemble a team of professionals who will work on your behalf to develop and implement a holistic financial, investment, and legacy plan.

The complexity of your current situation will demand more or less from each professional, but each is necessary to maximize your chance of success and limit the risk of failure. Make sure each professional is experienced, has fiduciary responsibility, and has the temperament to work as part of a team that puts your interests first.

You may wish to ask friends and family for referrals and conduct an interview with a questionnaire to help you determine if their business model meets your needs and expectations. Appendix A offers a questionnaire to ask financial advisers. Appendix E is a questionnaire to ask estate planning attorneys. Try to interview at least three professionals so you can determine who is most experienced in handling what is important to you and how he or she can be instrumental in helping you achieve your financial goals.

Personal Biases

Every person is an amalgamation of everything he or she has experienced, and considering each person's unique DNA, these experiences will differ in his or her decision-making efforts. Differing values, priorities, beliefs, etc., shape our future. I will cover some of the cognitive biases people have and how they relate to their personal finances. I do not pretend to be an expert in cognitive dissonance, so the examples and outcomes are elementary but can help explain why people make certain decisions and then wonder why they did so in the first place.

Most people believe they make good choices when buying items for themselves and their family. At some point, when the garage or storage shed is filled with unwanted and sometimes even unused items, they realize that their "impulses" got the better of them. When you see so many items at the consignment shops and secondhand stores that have the original tags still on them, you are glad you are not the only one.

In this example, the conflict is between our belief that we make good choices and that we believe we know what we need in order to be happy. Everyone wants to believe he or she makes good choices, and in fact most people sincerely believe they do. The cluttered closets, storage sheds, storage units (total rentable space as of the end of 2010 in the United States was 2.22 billion square feet, or an area more than three times the size of Manhattan in New York City [Self Storage Association, 2010]) and garages across the world show a different story; most people buy impulsively, and retailers understand this all too well, locating items *most needed* at the rear and sides of the store with a lot of items that people *want* in the middle and near the registers. So most people leave the store with more items than they originally intended to buy. This is why most consumers should write a shopping list and stick to it as much as possible. Doing so will help reduce the chances of falling prey to impulse buying. It will ideally leave more money in your pocket and probably help you reach your financial goals as well.

Now let's begin the discussion of cognitive bias as it relates to the financial world. In its truest sense, cognition is defined as a logically based process you perform when making a decision. Since the process is logical, emotion and one's own will are excluded. So, how do we "logically" make a decision? Again, it is not as easy as it may appear at first glance because there are so many biases that we may not even know exist. I will highlight a few of them to give you a flavor and why, for most people, it is difficult managing their financial assets.

Confirmation Bias

One bias that could be one of the many reasons for family arguments is "confirmation bias," which is the tendency to filter information to retain only what conforms to one's preferences and to reject everything else. In other words, if the information agrees with your opinion, it must be right and if it disagrees with your opinion, it must be wrong and therefore discarded. Stubbornness is an outcome of such a bias. You may have heard the phrase "diversification reduces risk." During turbulent, volatile markets, diversification is difficult to achieve because the "normal" correlation between asset classes is no longer "normal." Buying stocks from domestic, international, and emerging markets that are declining/rising in value at the same time is not necessarily better than buying just one of the asset classes. Anyone who has been invested during past bear/bull markets can relate. Warren Buffett has said that "diversification is only for those who do not know what they are doing." Not all of us have Mr. Buffett's talent, so diversification is more prudent than not doing so, but it will not be a complete solution.

Semmelweis Reflex

The second bias that may be interfering with sound financial decision-making is what is known as the Semmelweis reflex. It occurs when you automatically reject facts when they conflict with entrenched ideas or beliefs, not necessarily your own. Allocating your portfolio based on your age is such an example.

For instance, if you are fifty-five years old, it says you should allocate 55 percent of your portfolio to fixed income investments such as bonds, certificates of deposit, and cash equivalents, while 45 percent of your portfolio should be in equities. Since this is a macro-asset allocation strategy, it does not take into account your personal situation, risk tolerance, or current market conditions. With interest rates as low as they are now (in 2012), how can your overall portfolio meet your total return expectations? Put pencil to paper and figure it out. So, hypothetically, if your fixed income portion provides a 3 percent annual return for the next decade, the equity portion of your portfolio would have to return nearly 15 percent per year to meet an 8 percent compounded total return goal (assuming 1 percent asset management and/or fund fees). At that rate, the Dow Jones Industrial Average would be close to 45,000 by 2022 – a quadrupling in just 10 years!

For another example, look at the United States' current debt situation. Our elected officials have increased the debt ceiling more than seventy times (Austin and Levit, 2011) since the Second Liberty Bond Act was passed by Congress in 1917. Debt must be good, since the United States is the largest economy in the world and the US dollar is the world's reserve currency, right? Well, with the advent of the TEA ("Taxed Enough Already") Party in the past few years and our absolute level of debt, this entrenched idea that debt is good for long-term growth is coming under pressure. The solution to this example of the Semmelweis reflex will not be easy as our political leaders are staunchly Partisan.

Outcome Bias

Outcome bias occurs when you evaluate the quality of a decision when the outcome of that decision has already occurred. For example, you bought a home in 2006 because lenders were offering mortgage loans with no money down; the cost of owning a home was within your budget; you were with your current job for three years; you and your wife were expecting an addition to your family; and renting an apartment was not in your long-term plans. You worked with a real estate agent who was knowledgeable about the areas that have good public schools, favorable crime statistics, an abundance of local parks, and quality restaurants. You kept your total mortgage payment to 30 percent of your income and purchased a three-bedroom, two-bath "starter" home for $300,000. Housing prices have risen steadily for the past thirty years and interest rates are low by historical standards. Seems to be a no-brainer decision, doesn't it? Well, we all know what happened beginning in 2006. If we evaluate the quality of the decision at the time it was made, it was a good decision. If we evaluate it using 2012 standards and knowledge, it wasn't. So for this example, outcome bias would say this had been a bad decision when in fact it had been a good decision at the time the decision was made.

Normalcy Bias

Normalcy bias occurs when someone makes a decision without determining the possibility of future loss and their reaction if that loss does happen. Continuing from our previous example, housing prices in the United States as a whole had never decreased as much as they did from 2007 to 2008 since the Great Depression. So, many people and even the ratings agencies such as Moody's Analytics, Standard & Poors, and Fitch did not see the crash of housing prices as a probability or even a possibility. Without factoring this into their financial models, ratings of residential mortgage-backed securities (RMBS) were higher than they should have been, and purchasers of the RMBS paid higher prices than their intrinsic value. Since this situation had never occurred since the advent of RMBS, no one had adequately planned for such a disaster and was unable to determine the possible ramifications on the entire financial services industry. To make matters worse, there was no tried and true method to get us out of the situation. When something occurs that is not foreseen because it has never happened before, even the best laid plans can be turned upside down. It is important to be nimble and to try and avoid "bubbles" in your financial affairs.

Money Illusion

Money illusion was first introduced by John Maynard Keynes in the early twentieth century (Fisher, 1928). He believed people thought too much about the nominal value (denomination) of money and not enough about its real value (purchasing power). In a world with so many different currencies, your purchasing power depends upon the exchange rate of your local currency to the currency of the products origin. If the US dollar has weakened over the past decade when compared to the Australian dollar, you would need more US dollars to buy a product made in Australia than you did a decade ago. If you take a vacation to Australia in a few years and believe the US dollar will weaken between now and then, you can preserve the purchasing power of your money by converting your US dollars to Australian dollars now.

Anchor Bias

Finally, one must be able to determine the importance of different components in the decision equation. Anchor bias occurs when one places too much weight on one piece of information or belief when making a decision. Many investors purchase large amounts of stock in the company they work for because they are familiar with the company culture, its products and services, and its market position. Over time, this familiarity becomes comfort and then comfort becomes an anchor. Imagine all those people who put a large portion and, for some, all of their retirement plan assets into Enron, Worldcom, or small companies such as Stone and Webster.

Another example of anchor bias is whether someone is a staunch optimist or pessimist. The optimist always believes the markets will come back and is willing to accept large fluctuations in their account values. The pessimist believes the opposite, thinking gloom and doom is always on the horizon. Both are right at different times, so each can make money over periods of time, but in most circumstances, both cannot make money during the same time period. A realist, on the other hand, is free to change from a favorable to a non-favorable viewpoint and vice versa when conditions change. Consequently, realists are capable of making money whether the markets are going higher or lower.

Cognitive biases as described above are normal human traits. Understanding them and being able to apply what you have learned is not, and it will help you make better, less emotional decisions.

Section Three—Big Picture

Imagine if you could do whatever you wanted without concern for money. Would you be doing what you are doing now? Does your future include at least a few of those dreams? If not, you need a plan to help get you there. Your current situation is a result of the choices you have made so far in your life. Some have had more opportunities than others, but this book focuses on what you can do from this point forward.

With liberty and freedom comes the ability to amass great wealth and to also live in poverty. There are more than ten million millionaires in America today with that number projected to double by the year 2020 (Freeman and Srinivas, 2011). On the opposite side of the spectrum, nearly one in six Americans now live at or below the poverty line, with more than forty million receiving food stamps. That number is projected to grow, but thankfully not as quickly. The rich are getting richer and the poor are getting poorer. This is the story of the great divide that began many years ago between the "haves" and "have-nots," and we will have to address it, as a sovereign nation, in the near future.

For the "have-nots," the demands on your checkbook and time may have you feeling "locked in" with nowhere to go. The economy is sputtering and the outlook is not much better. Your paycheck doesn't seem to go as far as it did a few years ago, and gasoline, food, utility, and entertainment prices just keep increasing. You have cut back on many nonessentials but still have difficulty saving and ultimately investing. Financial stress is always there, looking at you in the mirror every morning. What can you do to change that? First by reading this book, second by developing a plan, and third by committing to working your plan. Sounds easy enough, but it will be a difficult process that discourages many and will take many years to successfully complete.

For the "haves," your income is sufficient for meeting your needs and many of your wants, and you even have money left over to invest. Your investments took a major hit during the financial crisis of 2007–2009 and you are concerned about the US debt situation, Europe, et al., and their effects on your bottom line. Keeping what you have is vitally important so you don't become one of the "have-nots." Your game-plan should focus on mitigating the effects of risk, taxes, and inflation.

Each begins at a different place, and hopefully each will end up at the same place—financial freedom.

CHAPTER TWO

▽

Finding Your Balance

Moderation, which consists in indifference about little things, and in a prudent and well-proportioned zeal about things of importance, can proceed from nothing but true knowledge, which has its foundation in self-acquaintance.
—Plato

Or as William Shakespeare so aptly wrote in Hamlet, "To thine own self be true." What is Polonius trying to say to his son, Laertes? I believe he was trying to impart some wisdom learned from years of self-neglect that being a debtor or a lender, carousing with women of questionable character, and other such pursuits is not being true to your "self." Instead, those pursuits lead to a poor reputation, financial distress, and, ultimately, despair. Only if you are true to yourself, taking care of your responsibilities, can you be in a position to be a blessing to others.

Section One—
Finances, Family and Friends, and Faith

How important are each of the "four Fs" to you? Try to prioritize them and spend time and effort accordingly. Developing this "budget" will help keep you on the right track and also increase the quality of time you spend on each. This is extremely important when you have a spouse and family as demands for your time and money are very high. Please see Appendix B as a guide to help you get started.

Finances

Finances are important because we are dependent upon our ability to purchase items we need to survive, such as food, clothing, and shelter. Our nation has transformed from a rural, agrarian economy into an urban, service-oriented one, and as a result, become more interdependent. This interdependency has changed the culture of families, and our response to that change is evident in our standard of living. We are a nation of specialists, working together as breakneck speed, to obtain __. You can fill in the blank with those things that are important to you and your family.

Family and Friends

Family and friends help us cope with the everyday stresses of life as we share our joys and heartaches of relationships, jobs, and events. All of us need someone to talk to once in a while and to be with to share experiences. For some, like yours truly, immersion in reading books or watching movies and TV seems normal, while others feel more comfortable being around large groups of people. Neither is better than the other, just different. Recognizing who you are more comfortable being and letting your friends and family know that it's your idiosyncrasies and not their behavior that limits your interactions is definitely worth sharing. At least they know it's you and not them!

Faith

Our nation was founded on the principles of Christian values and our founding fathers' dependence upon their faith is evident in the Declaration of Independence, the Constitution, and in the many books and articles they authored. I believe the United States of America has been blessed by God as a result of such faith and provided us with the ability, and, yes, the responsibility to be a blessing to others. Our ability to share our values has improved the world, but we need to remember the importance of liberty and freedom. My favorite line in the Declaration of Independence is, "And for the support of this declaration, with a firm reliance on the protection of divine providence, we mutually pledge to each other our lives, our fortunes, and our sacred honor." It clearly states their resolute faith as the foundation of their action. Your faith should also be the foundation for your values as you grow in wealth and become better able to help those less fortunate.

Section Two—
Designing Your Lifestyle: Now versus Later

That's right; design your lifestyle. You have the authority to do so. Change, when following a plan, can improve your chances of fashionably living within your means.

Stop to think about that for a minute.

I did not say that change can necessarily bring happiness. Rather, the process can help you realize what is important to you and your family and have the ability to then create a new lifestyle. So how do you define "lifestyle? I generally define it as "living one's personal values."

Your values are based upon parental guidance, your religious faith, personal experiences with your friends and family, and even what you watch on TV. They are part of you and help you make decisions, affect your behavior, and are the basis of your character. A few examples of values are integrity, honesty, credibility, dignity, stewardship, wisdom, accountability, fairness, generosity, dependability, compassion, and security.

When you combine your values with those of your family, a "family culture" is created. Opposing values can create a volatile relationship, so it is vital to understand the values of each member of your family so you can understand "where they are coming from". Only then can you effectively communicate and build a winning team.

Now that you and your family are on the same page (seriously, this is important), you have the ability to create a lifestyle that will reduce familial stress and improve your mental wellbeing.

At this point, some clients are lost and may be in the process of having a cerebral hemorrhage. They are so busy with all of their current responsibilities, have been "in a rut" for many years, and have no idea how to "succeed" in this area of their life. This is where a lifestyle coach may enter the picture as part of your advisory team. A professionally trained, experienced lifestyle coach will help you determine your personal/professional goals and provide education and motivation to help you achieve those goals.

Again, this is a process and will take time and introspection. Please see Appendix C for a lifestyle-planning worksheet.

By designing your new, current lifestyle with a time and money budget, you are on your way toward having the resources available to design your retirement lifestyle. There are no guarantees, of course, but the process is what is most important. Remember, to thine own self be true.

▽

CHAPTER THREE

Understanding Change
and Embracing It

Every trial endured and weathered in the right spirit
makes a soul nobler and stronger than it was before.
—James Buckham

You have probably heard the adage that "pain builds character." Well, that can be true if you learn from the experience. In the financial world, I believe that financial pain *reveals* character. When one has his or her back to the financial wall, how does he or she respond and why? For example, the housing bubble of 2002–07 created the illusion that buying a house would create instant wealth. When the bubble burst, many new homeowners (and those who took out equity) were upside down (owed more on the home than it was worth). Even though they are able to pay the monthly mortgage, many purchased a similar home and then let their existing homes go into the foreclosure process. This is called "strategic default." Both houses will be paid off in thirty years (all else being equal), but the "strategic defaulter" will have saved tens if not hundreds of thousands of dollars by breaking a contract they have the capacity to perform. This "cost" is borne by the others who decide to keep paying on their mortgages and is built into the cost and availability of future mortgage products.

Section One—Marriage/Divorce

According to Jennifer Baker of the Forest Institute of Professional Psychology, 50 percent of first marriages, 67 percent of second marriages, and 74 percent of third marriages end in divorce (Divorce Statistics). Allaboutfamilies.org reports that 95 percent of all divorced people eventually remarry, and 76 percent of those marriages fail in the first five years. These statistics show a pattern that clearly defines the problem: some people are just not suited (or prepared) for marriage.

When two people enter into the bonds of holy matrimony, there are many financial questions and, consequently, many potential problems. Since most marriages end because of financial problems, I would suggest you meet with your financial adviser *before* you tie the knot so you have an understanding of what financial elements (beliefs, spending patterns, debts, assets, etc.) will be brought into the marriage and their corresponding responsibilities.

Before you meet with your financial adviser, run credit reports for each person and go through them together to make sure they are accurate. This way you can see the history of accounts, balances, payments, and, most important, the credit score for each person. If there are any inaccuracies, you can contest them and have them corrected by writing letters, etc. Check the Federal Trade Commission's (FTC) website (http://www.ftc.gov/bcp/edu/pubs/consumer/credit/cre13.shtm) for more information about how to order your free credit report, understanding your legal rights, and repairing your report if it's inaccurate or incomplete. Additionally, you are entitled to a free credit report annually from each of the three credit reporting agencies. Visit annualcreditreport.com for more information.

Next, it is important to understand each spouse's financial values. By values, I don't mean amounts but rather which financial areas have "value or importance" to you. Please see Appendix G for a financial values worksheet. Have each spouse complete the worksheet independent of the other, without consideration for what you feel the other spouse would prefer. Now that each has completed their worksheet, compare them and determine where you have common ground and where you differ. If you have many differences, it is important that you resolve them before marriage rather than let it define your marriage. Meeting with an adviser, pastor, and even discussing it with your family and friends can help provide a framework from where you can begin the process of negotiation. This framework is the foundation upon which you will build your financial house.

Next, create a family budget. Appendix F is provided to help you get started. Creating a budget is a time-consuming task, so be sure to spend the time now.

Section Two—Baby

If you are having a child or already are a parent, congratulations! Expecting a child is an exciting and nervous time for most parents. The thoughts of how your life will change can be both stimulating and debilitating. Imagining the fun times you will have taking them to the zoo, teaching them how to read, seeing their face when they try new foods, tucking them in at night, and smiling when they have more fun playing with the box than the toy. Thinking about how you can provide for all of their needs until they are capable of taking care of themselves is another matter. There are some basic things you need to do.

1. Make sure your health insurance provider knows you have another member of your household. Verify that the policy covers dependents and that the cost is reasonable for the services that are covered. Well-

baby care is extremely important, so read your policy carefully and coordinate care with your pediatrician.

2. Now that you have more fiscal responsibility, determine the proper level of life insurance you need. A financial-needs analysis update is recommended. Adding additional term life insurance (twenty- to thirty-year-level term) coverage for both spouses is the least expensive way to transfer financial risk.

3. Consider adding an umbrella liability policy to augment your homeowner's policy, if you don't already have one. Children are prone to accidents, and having insurance to cover their costs seems prudent.

4. Begin the discussion of a college savings plan. There are many different types of plans available and they vary by state, so do your research and determine which plans seem reasonable for your budget and that provide the opportunity for others (friends and family) to contribute to directly. College may seem far away, but it will be right around the corner before you know it. This is covered in more detail in Chapter Six.

5. Make sure basic estate planning issues are addressed. Designate a legal guardian for your child(ren) and make sure the guardian understands the implications and responsibilities. If you don't have a will and/or living will, create one now. Update beneficiary designations, and, since minors cannot legally own any assets, make sure to appoint a guardian you believe will be responsible for distribution of assets as needed. In addition, you may consider a living trust and/or Castle Trust. Interview at least three qualified estate planning attorneys before deciding what makes the most sense

for your family. Appendix E is provided to help you with that process.

Section Three—Empty Nest

When our last daughter leaves home, my wife and I will definitely differ on the emotional aspects. She will probably be crying and experience separation anxiety (maybe even months in advance). I, on the other hand, will be sad to see her leave, but with a sense of relief and accomplishment. Welcome to the "empty nest."

Now that you have a lot more time on your hands and probably fewer expenses (unless your children live in distant cities and you and/or your spouse visit them too often), what do you do?

In our case, they just opened a new community center a few blocks away that has exercise classes (yoga, Zumba, Pilates, etc.), hands-on art classes (painting, sculpting, drawing, etc.), photography lessons, scrapbooking, and many others. Most cost only a few dollars or are free. My wife is already trying out some classes and likes Zumba so much that she may even become a certified instructor. The local university (University of New Mexico, my alma mater—Go Lobos!) also has a community college arm with classes in many subjects including cooking, astronomy, woodworking, and home decorating. They also sponsor day trips to many locations in the state and are reasonably priced. With Albuquerque being at the foot of the Sandia and Manzano mountains, there are hiking trails, picnic areas, and plenty of other outdoor activities that are just waiting for us. So many possibilities.

Now is also the time for many to step up their contributions to their retirement plans. You are probably in your peak earning years, so figuring out your retirement income needs is a basis for how much and how long you need to save and invest. If you are working with professional advisers, be sure that you agree with the assumptions they are using to forecast growth, tax rates, inflation, and spending. If possible, have them run "what-if" analysis to stress test your retirement income plan so you feel comfortable that you will be able to retire on your terms. As I said earlier, determine how much risk you need to take, not how much risk you want to take, so the probability of reaching your retirement goal is greater.

Also, it is recommended you begin to determine your need for long-term care insurance if you haven't already. This will be covered in more detail in Chapter Nine.

Finally, I would recommend spending more time with your spouse. Reconnecting with why you fell in love and got married all those years ago can rejuvenate your spirit as well as strengthen your dependence upon each other. I'm sure you can find common ground on activities you can do together. Some spouses need more "space" than others, so make sure they have some alone time.

An empty nest may sound lonely, but most of my clients find they are just as busy, if not more so, during this period of their lives. Just figuring out what to do is the difficult part as there are so many choices.

Section Four—Career Change / Layoff

When one spouse loses their job, what do you do? Hopefully, you already have a financial plan in place and have the basics such as an emergency fund, a working family budget, proper insurances, and well defined goals. This will reduce the amount of stress during the transition and allow you the opportunity to celebrate all the hard work and commitment to the plan you have done over the years. Yes, celebrate. Those who didn't plan for such an eventuality are usually only a paycheck or two away from financial devastation and their anxiety is off the charts. After your brief celebration (maybe a nice family dinner or short vacation; whichever you can afford without adding more stress/

anxiety), there are a few things that may help during the job hunting process.

First, set an appointment with your spouse to discuss changes needed to weather the revenue shortfall. Look at your family budget and reduce non-essential items wherever possible. Work with your financial planner to coordinate the changes to your financial plan. This type of communication is essential. Without it, you may deplete your savings faster than necessary.

Second, apply for unemployment benefits. The amount you receive will be dependent upon your previous salary. The duration will depend upon government policies at the time of your application.

Third, purchase temporary health insurance, if not included in your severance package. If you leave your job, or are fired/laid-off/downsized from your position, you are entitled, under federal law, to continue receiving your health benefits. Under the Consolidated Omnibus Budget Reconciliation Act (COBRA), employers with 20 or more employees must give departing employees the option of continuing their health coverage at the worker's own expense (plus an administrative fee) for up to 18 months – including family coverage. Your employer is *required* to give you COBRA benefits paperwork when you leave your position. You may be able to negotiate a lower rate in exchange for a higher deductible. If you continue to be unemployed after 18 months or if the cost of the insurance is too high and you can qualify for new health coverage (no pre-existing conditions), you may wish to consider a temporary health plan. Otherwise, many states have programs that residents can purchase without restriction. Premiums may be higher, but taking the risk off the table is probably worth it.

Fourth, stop using your credit and debit cards whenever possible. Paying cash for everyday purchases helps people refrain from spending, especially when cash money is tight.

Fifth, dedicate your time to finding new sources of income. Depending upon your skills and assets, you may wish to open a new business or even work from home on a contract basis. Make sure your Linkedin biography is up to date and check out online job sites such as monster.com and careerbuilder.com. Local employment agencies have an incentive to connect you with an employer, so make sure you are on their list.

The fastest growing jobs for the next decade are projected to be in medical, technology, and finance, so consider going back to school. Try not to take out student loans as they can come back to haunt you later (we will discuss why student loans are a bad idea in the education planning section).

CHAPTER FOUR

▽

Risk

There is another serious problem I have seen everywhere—
savings are put into risky investments that turn sour, and
soon there is nothing left to pass on to one's son. The man who
speculates is soon back to where he began—with nothing.
—Ecclesiastes 5:13–14, (The Living Bible)

Risk is a four-letter word. Many people try to avoid as much risk as they can, but instead they should learn about the different types of risk, understand what types of risk they are comfortable with, and then develop and implement a plan that can help them reach their goals. There are many types of financial risk, including credit, interest rate, reinvestment, liquidity, market, inflation, systematic versus nonsystematic, and currency. Before we describe each one and its potential impact on your financial goals, let's educate ourselves about how risk is determined.

Section One—How Risk Is Determined

When a debtor (borrower) creates a loan agreement (a formal document that describes a loan), what are its terms dependent upon? Generally, the better the capacity of the debtor to pay the obligations of the loan, the lower the interest rate. So, what does "capacity" mean? Basically, it comes down to the ability and willingness of the debtor to meet its financial obligations. Loan agreements may include covenants (restrictions), collateral (something of value to back the loan, such a property or inventory), guarantees, financial reporting requirements (transparency of the debtor's financial situation), and terms (rate of interest, duration) at issue.

For most debt issues, a ratings agency studies the loan agreement and assigns a rating. The rating is their best guess as to the level of the issue's creditworthiness relative to others. So, a rating of A is better than B. As financial situations change, ratings agencies such as Moody's, Standard & Poors, and Fitch, can place an issue on notice of positive/negative watch and upgrade/downgrade an issue's overall rating.

If you buy debt, you are a lender. Debtors can be corporations, governments, churches, even your family and friends.

If a company doesn't want to be a debtor, they can choose to sell a portion of their company to raise money. Only companies can issue equity. Such equity offerings are complex, so I will not discuss them in detail. Essentially, the intrinsic value of a company is the discounted value (the value of earnings in the future is worth less today because of inflation, uncertainty, etc., so a discount rate is used) of all earnings projected for the company into the foreseeable future. The "fair value" per share of the company's equity is the discounted value divided by the number of outstanding (issued) shares. If traded on an exchange, the actual price of the equity will be different because it will be based on supply and demand.

If you buy equity, you are an owner.

Risk is an interesting topic because most people tend toward safety and certainty, albeit in differing degrees. Here is a story that you should be able to relate to:

Let's look at John, an investor who wants the best return he can get when investing in his retirement. He looks at the returns of the different asset classes of equities, fixed income, and cash for the past fifty years and likes the return that equities have provided over that period of time. He decides to purchase one stock as it will be easier to track and will not cost him any additional fees, expenses, or capital gains tax to hold the investment until he needs the money for retirement in thirty years. The stock, however, has many risks as his friendly broker, Hal, discusses with him: "John, are you aware of the risks?" John says yes. He tells Hal that the company he wants to purchase "has been in business since the mid-1800s and is one of the largest financial institutions in the world. If the price drops, it will do so only temporarily and will recover as it always has." After hearing John's line of reasoning, Hal asks, "Are you aware of any other type of risk you are taking?" John says, "No, not really." Hal then informs John of some of the risks, such as market risk, capital risk, currency risk, financial risk, and systematic versus unsystematic risk.

Feeling totally overwhelmed by risk of equities, John thanks Hal for the discussion and hangs up. Determined to find a less risky alternative with similar returns, John scours the internet. He learns about mutual funds and how they are professionally managed and diversified. Looking at the universe of more than ten thousand funds, John would like some help in picking the fund that may best help him reach his retirement goal. John calls Hal and informs him of his desire to purchase an equity mutual fund. Hal asks John if he is aware of the risks. John said that is why he likes mutual funds, because they are diversified and professionally managed. Hal agrees that mutual funds are probably a better investment vehicle than individual stocks for most novice investors, but they do have risks. In addition to the risks of individual equities, mutual funds also have diversification and manager risk.

John, somewhat discouraged but resolute in his desire to eliminate investment risk, comes across the safest investment he has ever heard of, a US government treasury bond. He quickly dials the phone (John still uses a rotary phone because he doesn't like change) to call Hal. John is upbeat and tells Hal about how he is comfortable with US government treasury bonds as they have no risk. He tells Hal that they have outperformed inflation over the past fifty years and would be his ticket to a comfortable retirement. Finally being able to get a word in edgewise, Hal asks John the same question as before: "John, are you aware of the risks?" John pauses and says, "You mean there is a risk?" Hal says, "Yes, John, there are many. Among those are credit risk, reinvestment risk, interest rate risk, and liquidity risk." Hal then proceeds to briefly describe each type of risk and asks John, "Which of these risks are you comfortable with?" Being obsessed with trying to avoid risk, John says, "None", but thanks Hal for their discussion.

Overcome with the feelings associated with risk, John decides to leave his money in cash at his local bank (there are risks there too). He doesn't know it yet, but in a few years John will begin to understand what Yogi Berra meant when he said, "A nickel ain't worth a dime anymore." This is called purchasing power risk.

The moral of the story is that you cannot entirely avoid risk. Rather, one risk can be substituted for another. You must know the risks you are taking and be comfortable knowing that all investors and savers are in the same situation—trying to get the best possible return for the least amount of risk. But when you try to avoid risk, ask yourself why and how can that help you reach your goal.

I have always believed that most investors are not prudent risk managers and make emotional decisions during volatile market conditions. Consequently, I always counsel clients that, "The more risk you take, the less likely you are to reach your goal." This will be discussed in more detail in the risk tolerance section below.

Section Two—Types of Investment Risk

There are many different investment vehicles (mutual funds, unit investment trusts, variable annuity separate accounts), but most are comprised of individual fixed income securities, such as bonds (corporate, municipal, treasury) or individual equities (common stock, preferred stock).

Individual Fixed Income Securities

To reiterate, this is for individual securities, not packaged products such as mutual funds, unit investment trusts, or annuities.

For individual fixed income securities, the major risks are:

1. Credit Risk—The risk that an issuer will default on an obligation. Risk can be mitigated by collateral.

2. Event Risk—The risk of regulatory changes or other external events that are unforeseen and of material impact. Certain industries and/or sectors can be targeted for specific regulations or litigation.

3. Liquidity Risk—The risk that an investor will not be able to buy or sell a security at favorable terms.

4. Call Risk—The risk that an issuer may, at his or her discretion, decide to retire an asset, in whole or in part, before the asset's final maturity date, when it would have been in the investor's best interest to not do so.

5. Extension (Prepayment) Risk—The risk that an issue may, at the discretion of the issuer, decide not to retire an asset, in whole or in part, before the asset's final maturity date, when it would have been in the investor's best interest to do so.

6. Deferral Risk—The risk of an issuer's right to delay (temporarily or indefinitely) payments of interest or dividends.

7. Currency Risk—The risk that a currency devaluation or exchange rate change will result in a change in the asset's value. This risk can be mitigated by swap agreements.

8. Interest Rate Risk—The risk that a change in interest rates will cause the value of an asset to decline.

9. Inflation Risk—The risk that inflation will erode the value of an asset over time.

10. Leverage Risk—The risk that a change in the cost of financing the issue's debt increases and thereby reduces the amount and the ability of the issuer to pay its obligations, thus leading to price volatility.

Individual Equities

For individual equities, the major risks are:

1. Market Risk (Systematic Risk)—The risk that is inherent in the entire market or market segment that you are investing in. You cannot "diversify away" systematic risk.

2. Issuer Risk (Unsystematic Risk)—The risk that an issuer of a security (or a security in the same industry/ sector) will not meet operating expectations.

3. Political Risk—The risk that occurs when a security's price is affected by political developments.

Section Three—Risk Tolerance

For many, this may be the most important part of this book as your financial future may depend upon it, so please read it slowly.

Now for the big question: "What is your risk tolerance?" There are many different questionnaires that can help you, but there is only one that has been scientifically proven correct. Why risk your financial future on a risk tolerance questionnaire that may not be accurate? That is why I have a commitment to best practices, so my clients have a better chance of achieving their financial, personal, and professional goals. By purchasing this book, I will provide you with *a risk profile analysis for free.* Just fill out Appendix D in its entirety and fax it to the number at the end of the questionnaire. Any and all information you provide is confidential.

Let's discuss risk tolerance from a different perspective. Instead of asking how much risk are you comfortable with, I help clients figure out how much risk they *need* to take to fulfill their financial obligations (there is that dreaded family budget again) and subsequently reach their financial goals. Taking more risk than you need to, especially in volatile markets, is usually not worth it. In fact, you may not reach your goals by taking more risk.

Let me explain with a very simple scenario using actual investment returns. Assume the goal is to have $25,000 available to send your child to college in five years. You have many investment choices, all with different risk profiles. Say the year is 1998 and your child will enter college in the fall of 2003 and you have budgeted $400 per month for the next five years to reach your goal. If you invest in a bank savings account that pays an average of 4 percent interest for the next five years, you would have $26,608. Even if interest rates dropped to zero (which they currently are for most savings accounts), you would still have $24,000. You look at the stock market and think, *Wow, look at that performance. I think I will invest in the S&P 500 Index instead.* So for the years 1998–2002 (assuming you invested $4,800 on Jan 1 of each year), you diligently follow your plan, but you would only have $18,290—not enough to meet your goal because you took more risk than necessary and invested when the equity markets declined.

Since most families have more than one financial goal, I recommend they prioritize their needs and goals and then determine the risk they can afford to take to meet each need and goal. In other words, for each goal, you need to determine the priority, set a timeframe, calculate an amount, and then determine how you will fund each goal, in that order. Going through this exercise should help you allocate your discretionary income more effectively, resulting in the most important goals having a higher probability of being met using a relatively lower risk investment strategy.

You may not be able to achieve every goal you have, but you now have a greater certainty of reaching the goal(s) with the highest priority and it is better to reach a few of your goals than to take a shotgun approach and not reach any.

Most advisers hand an investor a risk tolerance questionnaire (RTQ) from a product sponsor (mutual fund, annuity) or from a packaged planning system and use that RTQ to determine a proper asset allocation for your entire portfolio. You can see where this is heading; one size fits all. I believe that each investor should have goals-based portfolios with each goal having a unique risk tolerance, investment strategy, etc. In other words, each goal has a corresponding portfolio that is uniquely tailored and separately managed. You have heard that investment portfolios should be diversified (stocks, bonds, alternatives, cash), and now you know that you should have diversified (priority, certainty) goals-based portfolios.

CHAPTER FIVE

$\triangledown$

Planning Essentials

It pays to plan ahead. It wasn't raining when Noah built the ark.
—Anonymous

First you need to know *why* you're planning and secondly *what* you're planning for. The why will help define the what. Before the long-term planning process can begin, you need to have a workable budget, an emergency fund established, and proper insurance, so let's discuss those now.

Section One—Creating a Family Budget

If you are married or are sharing income and expenses with someone else, consider having each party create a budget (using Appendix F as a template), discuss the differences, and then create a consolidated budget (one that both parties can agree to and live by).

As you can see when using the budget template, expenses are segregated first by essential and discretionary and then by type. Essential expenses are those you are obligated to pay and that are necessary for survival. Common essential expenses are your mortgage/rent, utilities, food, transportation, and clothing.

For this exercise, determine what you can "make-do" with,

rather than what you currently spend money on. For example, if you are driving a luxury car with a $700 monthly payment, is that a necessity or more of a luxury? Can you "make-do" with a car that has a $300 monthly payment? Same is true for your living quarters, your cell phone plan, etc. So for purposes of filling out the budget for your cable television, write down in the essential expenses section the dollar amount for the plan that you can "make-do" with, and then the additional cost of the plan you would like to have in the discretionary expenses section. The same is true for each item on your list.

Your budget will only be as good as the time and effort you put in to it, so please take it seriously.

For most people, the viability of their long-term plans are dependent upon the budgeting process, so it is essential that you get this done properly and keep working at it at least annually and especially when there are big changes in your life (such as having a baby, getting a raise, health issues, etc.).

Section Two—Establishing an Emergency Fund

Yes, this is a "pool of money" that should only be tapped into for emergencies. It is not your savings account or part of your checking account. Instead, it is something that provides you with the ability to live for a period of time when something unexpected happens and your existing resources are insufficient to continue your planned lifestyle. You and I both hope you never need to use it, but it does provide peace of mind knowing it is there just in case.

Now comes the important question: Do you want your emergency fund to be *debt or equity*? For many families, it is difficult to save for let alone invest in the future. Trying to save to create an emergency fund sounds like a great idea, but it may not be practicable or even possible without sacrificing other financial goals. So let's explain what a *debt-enabled* emergency fund is and why it may benefit you in the short and long term.

Debt-enabled emergency funds are funded by—you guessed it—debt. Debt is created between a borrower and a lender and can be either secured or unsecured. Secured debt has some sort of collateral backing the loan, such as your car, house, 401(k), or business. Unsecured debt is based solely on your promise to pay it back, and as such, is a greater risk to the lender and has a higher interest rate because the lender may not receive anything in return if you cannot make your payments. Credit cards, personal loans, and loans from friends and family are some examples of unsecured debt. If you have a bad (low) credit score, your access to debt financing is severely restricted. Unfortunately, even if your credit score is good, access is still limited because of tighter lending standards and increased governmental regulation, but it is available, at a price. The price may include a fee for having access to a credit line, such as a home equity line of credit or an annual fee for a credit card. Either way, try to find sources of credit that have no annual fee; low, fixed interest rates; and a reasonable payment schedule. Only use your debt-enabled emergency fund when an actual emergency occurs.

The following question popped into my mind when I originally heard of this concept more than twenty years ago: "Why would someone want to have debt serve as their emergency fund?" And the answer is: "If the opportunity cost of using equity is too high."

For example, you need an emergency fund of $10,000 and you currently have the choice of saving $200 per month to create your emergency fund or investing that same money in your company retirement plan that has a 50 percent match up to the first 4 percent of your compensation. If you make $30,000 per year and are in the 15 percent tax bracket, the $200 you set aside for your emergency fund reduces your income by $200 and you would have $200 in your emergency fund account. If you invest the $200 in your company's retirement plan, your income would be reduced by $170 ($200 less tax savings of $30) and you would have $300 in your retirement plan account ($200 plus company match of $100). Most company-match contributions are subject to a "vesting" period (often five years), so take that into account as well.

So at the end of the first month, you have $30 more in your checking account and $100 more in assets (that grow tax deferred) if you fund your retirement plan instead of your emergency fund. If you continue to do so for the next four years and the accounts receive no interest, you either have $9,600 in an emergency fund or $1,440 in your checking account and $14,400 in your retirement plan. Which sounds better to you? Again, the correct answer is "it depends."

Since you do not know what the future holds, you must assign probabilities to certain factors (and others applicable to your personal situation), such as:

1. whether you stay with your employer long enough so the matching contributions are vested;

2. performance of the investments you selected in your plan;

3. having to use the funds for an actual emergency

Equity-enabled emergency funds are funded by assets. In the previous example, assume you deposit the $200 per month into a short-term, highly rated bond mutual fund that has check writing privileges. Interest rates are in the 1 percent range, so nothing to write home about, but it does provide daily liquidity and is "out of sight and out of mind." If you continue this for the next four years, you will meet your $10,000 goal and be ready to tackle your other financial goals. You are excited. Then you have a revelation regarding the current financial environment: "By earning only a 1 percent return on my money and with the inflation rate being a little more than 3 percent, I will have to continue to add to the emergency fund every year when the interest I receive is less than the rate of inflation." You think there must be a better way. Then you think, *Why not take a little more risk and invest in a balanced mutual fund?* You know where this is going—the risk/reward tradeoff. So if you want to assume more risk, make sure you can afford it.

So now that you have decided on either debt or equity as the mechanism for your emergency fund, how much should you set aside or have as a credit line? As with most financial questions, that depends upon many factors. Most advisers suggest an amount that will last for three to six months. I would go one step further and tailor it to your personal situation. To do so, consider the following factors: stability of your job (health of your employer and its industry); how long it takes for others with your skill set to find a new job; your health; size of your insurance deductibles; product warranties; maximum out-of-pocket expenses as outlined in your health insurance policy; importance of "discretionary" expenses; and fixed versus floating rate loans. As you can see, the budget you created is the basis for your emergency fund. All the more reason to look at that budget again and rework it as if you were unemployed or underemployed for an extended period of time.

It is important to note that an emergency fund should be tailored to your expenses, not your income, unless you would like to continue to be able to fund your other goals, such as retirement, college tuition, etc.

What really matters is that you have an emergency fund plan, one that is based on your risk tolerance, access to credit, company retirement plan, prevailing interest rates, and wealth and generosity of your friends and family. In other words, determine your personal "financial flexibility" first.

Section Three—Insurance

Many people think that insurance is merely a risk-transfer vehicle; you pay premiums in exchange for an insurance company's promise to pay an insured claim. To me, it means so much more. It provides me with the *ability to prevent unintended consequences.*

Imagine if your spouse (or even ex-spouse) is diagnosed with Alzheimers and does not have sufficient long-term care insurance (long-term care insurance is briefly discussed in Chapter Nine – Healthcare). Some family members may feel compelled to provide care, but will have to sacrifice work, time with their family, and may even develop health problems of their own as a result. With adequate coverage, everyone has a choice and can focus their time and efforts on accomplishing those things that are important to them.

As with all insurance companies you do business with, you want them to make a profit (reasonable) so they have the capacity to make good on their promises. When evaluating insurance companies, make sure you know their ratings and Comdex Ranking. There are four major independent third-party rating agencies for insurance companies: Moody's, Standard & Poor's, Fitch, and A.M. Best Company. Each agency evaluates the insurance company's financial statements and management (quantitative and qualitative) and the result is then compared to other insurance companies and a rating is established. The Comdex is not a rating, but a composite of all ratings the insurance company has received on a percentage scale of 1 to 100. I only recommend companies with a Comdex Ranking of 90 or better.

There are many types of insurance, but as a consumer, your goal should be the same: to reduce your risk of loss (financial and emotional) to a manageable level. Since most people pay more in premiums than they will receive in benefits (i.e., insurance company profits), it makes sense to match your coverage to your needs and review your coverage with your insurance professional(s) annually.

Insurance is divided into two main categories, property and casualty; and life, health, and disability.

Property and Casualty Insurance

Property insurance covers real assets, such as your home, automobile, and business, from loss or loss of income producing abilities. Casualty insurance protects a person from legal liability for losses caused by injury to others or damage to the property of others.

Most consumers know about auto and homeowners insurance so I will not go into the particulars of those policies. Unfortunately, most do not know what their coverage is or what is covered. Please review your auto and homeowners policies with your agent at your next opportunity.

One casualty insurance policy that is not as well-known but should be is an umbrella liability policy. It covers liabilities that are in excess of the limits of your auto, business, homeowners, or other types of policy and is generally much less expensive because it only "kicks in" after the limits of the other policies have been reached. Umbrella policies cover not only your current assets but your future earnings from potential loss. For example, if you cause damage to a third party and do not have enough insurance and assets to cover the expenses, a court could rule that a portion of your future wages could be garnished until the claim against you has been paid. Umbrella policies can also provide coverage for personal liability claims such as slander, libel, wrongful eviction, defamation, and many other potential claims such as liability arising from your service on the board of directors of your church or local charitable organization.

If you are thinking about purchasing an umbrella policy, make sure to give plenty of thought to what you have to lose, namely your assets and future stream of income. After you have come up with a realistic number that you want to protect from liability claims, you need to determine what kinds of liabilities you want to have insured. Finally, make sure to understand the provisions of the policy, especially those that deal with event triggers and duties. Here is a checklist that may help you through this process.

1. Is the insurance professional you are meeting with a captive agent (represents only one company) or an independent agent (represents many companies)? If he or she is a captive agent, make sure to meet with others so you have the means to compare coverages and quotes.

2. What are the total value and type of assets you are trying to protect?

3. Who will be responsible for monitoring this in the future?

4. Does the umbrella policy cover only those liabilities covered by existing (business, auto or property) insurance, or does it expand your coverage to things that are excluded in your existing policies?

5. What are the potential liability-causing occurrences offered by the umbrella policy?

6. Any restrictions?

7. Are you required to maintain coverage in certain amounts in your existing policies in order to meet the threshold of the umbrella coverage? If so, what are the amounts and who will be responsible for monitoring them in the future?

8. Does the umbrella policy provide for legal defense?

What about instances that are not indemnified under the policy?

9. What is the company's record of paying claims?

10. What is the company's rating?

11. Is the company in good standing with insurance regulators?

12. Any adverse press reports about the company?

13. Ask for a quote accompanied with any company brochures, sample coverage statements, and policies that are available. Keep these in your file for future reference.

Life, Health, and Disability Insurance

Life Insurance

Life insurance has become a complex financial instrument. Changes to the tax laws and innovative strategies devised by insurance companies have resulted in an explosion of uses for life insurance. For most readers of this book, life insurance should be used solely to offset the risk of losing a breadwinner's income stream due to a premature death. In addition, term life insurance is generally the most affordable method of insuring against this type of loss.

If you hear an insurance or other financial professional stating that life insurance is an investment, be careful. As in all "permanent" life insurance policies that have a cash value component, the cash value is considered an "overpayment" of the cost for the insurance component. If the insurance company has the right to raise premiums, the cash value component can be tapped if necessary, and even require you make additional premium payments in the future or the policy may lapse. Some include no-lapse guarantees for an additional cost.

I could write an entire book about the pros and cons of life insurance and its potential use in a financial plan, and I may do so someday, but my point is that life insurance is life insurance. If you treat it as anything else, be careful and have your professional thoroughly discuss "the worst that could happen."

Health Insurance

Most employees do not have an individual health or disability insurance policy. Instead, they rely upon their company to provide this type of coverage at lower group rates. If you are not covered by your employer for health and/or disability insurance or would like higher coverage, you would need to apply for an individually underwritten policy. You may be surprised at the cost when you are given a quote, as premiums have risen steeply in recent years. For our purposes here, I will briefly discuss what you should look for when getting a quote for individual insurance coverage.

When discussing health insurance, there are two main types of access to medical care, the health maintenance organization (HMO) and the preferred provider organization (PPO). The HMO is managed through your primary care physician and you see him or her first for treatment and/or for a referral to another doctor or specialist. HMOs generally provide broader coverage than PPOs and charge higher premiums. Under the PPO plan, you are responsible for managing your care because you can seek treatment from any doctor you choose as long as he or she is an approved provider (unlike an HMO you can also seek treatment from out-of-network physicians, but you will pay a greater portion of the cost). PPOs generally provide access to more physicians and treatment options than a typical HMO.

So which is better? Again, that depends on your budget, access to physicians you think you may need, limitations on coverage, and many other factors. Seems every state has different plans, so you need to work with your insurance professional to determine what type of plan is best for you and your family. Plans and options are always changing, so make sure to review plans annually and especially when your needs change.

When you apply for an individual health insurance policy, you will often be medically underwritten. The application will ask for details on your medical history, risk factors (smoking, weight, age, family health history, etc.), coverage limits desired, and many other variables. An underwriter is assigned to determine whether you are an acceptable risk, and if so, the premium you pay and the coverage provided will be determined by the underwriter based upon your perceived needs and health risks. This process is similar to applying for a loan, as the interest rate you are charged for borrowing money is dependent upon your perceived capacity to pay it back. This includes such factors as your credit history, current earnings, debt to income ratio, etc.

If you belong to any professional associations or organizations, check to see if they offer group policies for their members. This is especially helpful if you have pre-existing conditions and/or want a policy that has a national footprint.

If you are uninsurable, most states have an insurance plan available to cover you and the premiums are partially subsidized by the government so they may be more affordable.

With the recent passage of the Patient Protection and Affordable Care Act, please view the following website for detailed information: www.healthcare.gov.

Disability Insurance

Most of the families I have spoken with during my career only carry disability insurance through their employer's group plan. Here are some issues to think about before meeting with your insurance professional.

1. Do you want "own occupation" or "any occupation" coverage?

2. Who determines your "functional capacity" to perform your or any occupation?

3. If you change occupations and you have "own-occupation" coverage, do you need to notify the insurance company? If so, whose responsibility is it to do so and what potential affects does that have on the coverage?

4. Do you want "residual" benefits (covers partial disability)?

5. What is the process for filing a claim?

6. Does your policy pay for training and/or education if you are unable to continue performing work duties with your existing skills?

7. How long do you need the coverage to last?

8. How long do you want to be without coverage (elimination period)?

9. Do you want the coverage to have an inflation component (cost of living adjustment)? If so, what rate?

10. Can the policy be changed or cancelled by the insurance company?

11. Can the premiums be increased?

Since disability occurs more frequently than premature death for those younger than age sixty-five, premiums for the coverage are higher than those of term life insurance and may even seem expensive. It will only seem expensive until you need it. According to the Social Security Administration (Fact Sheet March 18, 2011) there is a three in ten chance that a twenty-year-old will become disabled before reaching retirement age.

You may not realize it, but 90 percent of all disabilities are caused by illness while only 10 percent are caused by accidents (Council for Disability Awareness, Long-Term Disability Claims Review, 2011).

Social Security has a disability component, and if you are eligible, it can provide for a nice benefit. In addition, those who qualify for Social Security Disability automatically get Medicare after two years even though they are younger than age 65. This program is in serious need of overhaul since it has paid out more in disability benefits than premiums received each year since 2005 (Wall Street Journal – March 22, 2011). Stay tuned for changes in eligibility and coverage. In the meantime, become familiar with Social Security disability coverage and determine your potential benefit by logging onto their website at *www.ssa.gov.*

CHAPTER SIX

▽

Education Planning

The only thing more expensive than education is ignorance.
—Benjamin Franklin

Having discussed the "first p"—preparation—let us now begin the "second p": planning. The Merriam Webster dictionary defines planning as "the act or process of making or carrying out plans; specifically: the establishment of goals, policies, and procedures for a social or economic unit." Let's break that down to its essential components. First, planning is an act or process, so you must *do* something. Second, it explains how you do it. Third, it says who you are doing this for. With that as our basis, most families focus on providing their children with a good education, having the ability to retire someday, and establishing a legacy.

There are many financial benefits for investing in an education savings plan for your children, including tax deferral, tax free distributions for qualifying expenses, penalty-free transferability, and even possible state tax deductions.

Section One—Custodial Accounts (UGMA/UTMA)

The Uniform Gift to Minors Act (UGMA) and Uniform Transfer to Minors Act (UTMA) are custodial accounts to hold and protect assets on behalf of a minor before the child reaches the age of majority in his or her home state. Such custodial accounts were used as the primary educational funding solution before the advent of Section 529 and 530 plans (see below in Section Two for more information). Any adult can set up a custodial account for any child younger than age eighteen, and there are not contribution limits (gift tax and estate tax exemption limits may apply; check with your financial adviser).

The assets in the custodial account are the property of the minor, but the custodian of the account (usually a parent or grandparent) has the responsibility of both investment and divestment of the account on behalf of the minor. Custodial accounts can be invested in such vehicles as stocks, bonds, mutual funds, annuities, and unit investment trusts (UITs) but are not allowed to invest in stock options or permitted to buy on margin. Any withdrawals from the account must be initiated by the custodian for the legitimate needs of the minor, not just college expenses.

For every child who is younger than age nineteen (twenty-four if a full-time student) and is claimed on the parents' tax return as a dependent, the first $850 of unearned income from dividends, interest, and realized gains in the custodial account is tax-free, the next $850 is taxed at the 10 percent level, and anything above that is taxed at the rate of the parents' tax bracket.

At the age of majority in the state where you live, the account becomes the sole property of the child and he or she has full control over the investments and how to use the funds. This is one potential disadvantage. The other is that custodial accounts negatively affect qualification for financial aid.

Section Two—Section 529 Plans

Section 529 of the Internal Revenue Code authorizes states, state agencies, or educational institutions to sponsor what are known as "qualified tuition plans." Such plans are tax-advantaged and were designed to encourage saving to pay for future college costs.

There are two types of Section 529 plans: prepaid tuition and college savings. Let's describe them briefly now.

Prepaid Tuition

Prepaid tuition plans were designed to mitigate the effects of inflation when planning for future college costs. In essence, it allows families to lock in tuition at current rates with no principal risk and many are backed by the full faith and credit of the state where the college is located.

Prepaid tuition plans are operated by state governments and their benefits vary widely. Since they are operated by the states, private colleges are not public institutions, so they are not covered. Most plans require that either the account owner (e.g., parent) or the beneficiary (future student) is a resident of the state when the account is opened. Once the account is opened, anyone can contribute to it. Prepaid tuition plans may be a good option for those families who may not qualify for needs-based financial aid.

The major benefits of prepaid tuition plans:

- They are guaranteed by the full faith and credit of the issuing state.

- They have a low impact on eligibility for needs-based financial aid.

- They have the ability to lock in future college costs at today's prices.

Some plans are being scaled back because of state budget cuts, so do your due diligence carefully.

College Savings Plans

College savings plans are similar in many ways to defined contribution retirement plans such as an IRA or 401(k). They are similar in that there are investment selections you need to choose from and that there is no guarantee that the amount you save will be sufficient to pay for college once that time comes. Some plans do not cover expenses for post-graduate degrees.

Anyone can contribute on behalf of a beneficiary, and with favorable gift tax treatment, it can be a good estate planning tool. Contribution limits and deductibility rules do apply, however, and vary by state. Series EE and I United States savings bonds issued after December 31, 1989, and Coverdell ESAs (named after late Senator Paul Coverdell [R-GA], are authorized by Section 530 of the Internal Revenue code and used to be called "Education IRAs." Coverdell ESAs provide a tax-advantaged investment account and were designed to encourage savings to cover future expenses for secondary and/or post-secondary education) may be redeemed tax-free if the proceeds are contributed to a Section 529 plan. Your tax adviser will know which forms you need to file.

Qualification for financial aid will depend upon rights to ownership of the 529 plan. Beginning in the 2009–10 school year, Section 529 plans, prepaid tuition plans, and Coverdell accounts are treated as parental assets if the child is a dependent.

The major benefits of a college savings plan are:

- high contribution limits;
- its low impact on eligibility for needs-based financial aid;
- the ability to use funds at any accredited post-secondary institution;
- flexible investment options and strategies

Some Commonalities between Prepaid
Tuition and College Savings Plans

- The account owner controls access to the funds.

- If the beneficiary doesn't go to college or the funds
  are used for other purposes, the account owner
  can redeem the account but may owe taxes and/or
  penalties to do so.

- Tax-deferred growth and tax-free withdrawals are
  offered if used for qualified higher education expenses.

- Section 529 assets are removed from the account
  owner's taxable estate.

- Contributions, up to the federal limit, are exempt
  from gift taxes.

- The account owner can rollover a 529 plan to a
  different 529 plan once per year, if desired.

- The account owner can change the beneficiary to
  another family member at any time if desired.

- Distributions from either type of Section 529 plan do
  not affect your qualification for other educational tax
  breaks such as the lifetime learning tax credit.

Section Three—
Coverdell Education Savings Accounts (Section 530)

How Coverdell ESAs are different from Section 529 plans:

- lower maximum annual contribution limits (currently
  $2,000 as of 2012)

- income limitation for contributors

- investments inside an ESA are the same as for IRAs

(can include stocks, bonds, mutual funds, unit investment trusts, CDs, etc.)

- ESAs have an expiration date. Balances must be used for qualified education expenses by the beneficiary's thirtieth birthday or transferred to a family member younger than thirty to avoid taxes and penalties.
- ESAs can be used for secondary and post-secondary education.

Section Four—US Savings Bonds

The US savings bond education tax exclusion allows qualified taxpayers the ability to exclude from their gross income all or a portion of the interest earned when they redeem eligible Series EE and I bonds issued after December 31, 1989, to pay for post-secondary tuition and other educational expenses at certain institutions.

The first step to qualify is that the purchaser of the bond must be at least twenty-four-years old before the issue date of the bond. Second, if your income is within certain limits, you may be eligible. Third, the expenses must be for the taxpayer, the taxpayer's spouse, or for the taxpayer's dependent. Fourth, the taxpayer must pay qualified education expenses equal to or greater than all proceeds from bonds redeemed during the year.

This may not be all the steps to qualify, but as you can see, the limitations are strict.

Section Five—Student Loans

The qualifications for student loans vary by provider and most are based on need. Loan terms are complex to understand for many students and should be explained fully by the lending institution before you commit to taking out the loan.

Earlier I wrote that student loans could come back to haunt

you later; well, here is the explanation: current student loan debt total of $1 trillion is greater than consumer credit card debt of $798 billion (Consumer Credit—G.19, 2012) as of February 2012, and if you get into a financial bind, student loans are not dischargeable in bankruptcy except in rare circumstances (including complete disability). For a website that describes the pros and cons of student loans very well, visit www.student-loans-digest.com.

Section Six—Grants

Every student would like to receive as many grants as possible because grants do not have to be paid back. They are, however, mostly awarded based on need, so many will not qualify. To determine if you do qualify for a federal grant, you will need to fill out the Free Application for Federal Student Aid (FAFSA) at www.fafsa.ed.gov. Make sure this is the website you use and do so over a secure connection. Priority deadlines are usually in mid-March for the next academic year, so give yourself the greatest chance at receiving a grant and complete the FAFSA and send it your educational institution by then.

Many organizations provide grants, so be sure to do your research, and be skeptical about providing your personal information before your due diligence is complete.

Education planning is a complex subject and should be coordinated with your financial planner, investment adviser, tax adviser, and estate-planning attorney.

CHAPTER SEVEN

▽

Retirement

Don't simply retire from something; have something to retire to.
—Harry Emerson Fosdick

Retirement, yes, but retired from what? For most it is that point in your life when you decide (or have someone else decide for you) to quit working for money and instead live on what you have earned, saved, and invested. For some it is a difficult transition, while for others it is merely opening a new chapter of his or her life that the retiree has already planned for.

With the shift from defined benefit plans (pensions) to defined contribution plans over the past three decades, many future retirees will have to make due with a "two-legged" stool, where the two legs are Social Security and personal savings. Without the traditional third leg of the stool—a company/government pension—it becomes even more important to have a plan that maximizes your chance of meeting your retirement goal. Some things you need to think about are investment choices, risk, and inflation.

Many employees have access to some sort of employer provided defined contribution plan, such as a simple IRA, 401(k), or 403b. Unfortunately, most plans only have a few investment choices to select from, so what can you do to make the most of a limited set of investment options? The answer is to manage all of your accounts as if they were one portfolio. For example, if your company plan only has one international equity alternative and its past performance has been dreadful, you should consider not investing in that fund and instead use money from other portfolios you may have to invest in that asset class, if you and your adviser feel it is prudent to do so at all. Do not manage each account separately. It is now possible for registered investment advisers to provide plan participants with individualized investment advice. There are some restrictions, so talk with your financial professional to see if they are qualified to provide this type of advice and if it is part of their business plan.

Section One—Frame of Mind

Retirement is a lifestyle, not a one-time event. Enough said.

Section Two—Usefulness and Importance

After many years of working, you have become a specialist at what you do, and you feel a sense of accomplishment. Many people have counted on you for your expertise, knowledge, and wisdom. You have probably helped many on their career paths by acting as a rudder during turbulent times. People have an innate need to feel useful and relevant. As a retiree, what can you do to get that feeling back again? Many decide to volunteer while others begin a second career, and others decide to just live it up as they have "put in their time." Hopefully, your choice is not dependent upon your financial situation, so let's tackle the major retirement planning concerns next.

Section Three—Concerns

Longevity

No one wants to run out of money before they run out of time. Some of us may remember when the checking account ran out before the end of the month and wondered how we could put food on the table, pay the utility bill, or put gas in the car. At least we had the comfort of knowing there was a paycheck around the corner.

During retirement, if your assets are depleted, that "paycheck around the corner" is probably limited to those sent to you by your family, friends, and the government. A very difficult position to be in, and one that everyone wants to avoid. Longevity risk is the possibility that you outlive your investments.

Rising Costs

According to the Bureau of Labor Statistics (May 23, 2011), a grocery basket consisting of a loaf of bread, a gallon of milk, and a dozen eggs cost four dollars and sixty-seven cents in March of 2001, and six dollars and sixty-five cents in March of 2011. That is a 42 percent increase in just one decade. Other items that consumers use each day, have increased even faster. Gasoline, for example, is up nearly 150 percent during that same timeframe.

How do you define inflation? It is generally defined as the rate at which the prices of goods and services increase. I define inflation somewhat differently. I define inflation as the silent thief that erodes the purchasing power of your money. A weak currency is also a silent thief as it contributes, albeit indirectly, to inflation and also reduces the purchasing power of your money versus other nations. For those on a fixed income without liquid investable assets, inflation will erode their lifestyle over a very short period of time. For example, if inflation averages 3 percent per year, the value of a dollar will decline by a quarter in fewer than eight years and by more than half in only twelve years.

If you do not factor in the effects of inflation on your retirement distribution plan, your lifestyle will have to be reduced accordingly as there will not be enough money to fund all of your expenses. Locking in secure income streams from bonds, certificates of deposit, and immediate annuities remains the same until maturity, resulting in a loss of purchasing power over time as inflation rises.

Consequently, any retirement distribution strategy you and/ or your advisers develop should account for increased spending needs.

Market Uncertainty

Doesn't it always seem that the stock and bond markets are in a state of flux? Over the past fifty years, the United States has been involved in four wars (Vietnam, Persian Gulf, Afghanistan, and Iraq), experienced seven recessions, had bear market corrections of 20 percent or more ten times, and had treasury bill rates ranging from 0.00 percent (multiple dates in 2008) to 17.14 percent on December 11, 1980 (Federal Reserve Board). No wonder most investors are skittish to invest for the long term these days. Investing your life savings during such tumultuous times seems like sheer lunacy. What is one supposed to do?

First, embrace that you do not have a crystal ball and will make mistakes. Second, understand the teachings of this book and apply them to your situation. Third, develop a team of knowledgeable, experienced advisers. Fourth, pray for the best.

Sequence of Returns

This is interesting, and most investors feel they are always on the "wrong side" of this analysis. Since market returns are random, no one can predict exactly or even come close to what the market will return each year for the duration of your retirement. Such random returns can either produce positive or negative results.

During the accumulation phase, the sequence of returns is not as important because they tend to average out over time. For example, assuming you begin with $10,000 and add $1,000 at the beginning of each year, and you earn a negative 10 percent in year one, positive 20 percent in year two, and positive 5 percent in year three, and this pattern is repeated ten times (for a total of thirty years), you would end up with $99,848.57 or an average annual return of 4.44 percent. Now assume you reverse the investment returns (positive 5 percent in year one, positive 20 percent in year two and negative 10 percent in year three) and repeat this pattern for the next thirty years, you would end up with 93,650.82 or an average annual return of 4.15 percent.

During the distribution phase, however, it becomes much more important. For example, let's begin with $100,000 and withdrawal 6 percent ($6,000) each year. How long will the money last? If we assume the sequence of returns is the same as the first case above, it will last twenty-six years. For the second case, it would last thirty-three years. If you factor in inflation, the difference becomes even greater.

I will cover this in more detail in Chapter Eight, Distribution Planning.

Section Four—Spending Levels

Every retiree should know the different levels of his or her spending needs. For example, there are generally four levels as to how income can be spent.

First is the survival level. This is the minimum income you need to survive, not live. Costs for dining out, going to the movies, or paying for a gym membership, cable television, and vacations is not on this list. Remember back to the days of going to college?

That is what I am talking about! See Appendix F for a sample worksheet.

Second is the "getting by" level. This includes the survival level plus items such as wellness planning,

Third is the "easy street" level. This includes eating out, vacations, and many other discretionary items.

Fourth is the "philanthropy" level. Here is where you have all of your needs and wants met and still have money to bless others.

Section Five—Ways to Reduce Costs in Retirement

With the poor market performance of the past decade, underfunded pension plans, high unemployment, and projections for lower than normal economic growth for the foreseeable future, many Americans do not have the resources they thought they would at this time of their life (retirement). Beginning a personal austerity program is difficult but can be done. Again, see Appendix F for a budget worksheet and complete it as described in Chapter Two.

The following sections will provide you with a starting point.

Housing Expenses

Since housing expenses are usually the largest portion of one's budget, let's begin with ways you can save.

1. Downsize to a smaller home or one that has better amenities for your retirement needs in the area where you currently live. You already are familiar with local attractions, and costs for food, entertainment, and other services will remain the same. Consider distributing some of your estate (furnishings, heirlooms, etc.) to your heirs at this time.

2. Move to a more affordable location. If you have

children who have moved away, this option is much more appealing. Lower cost locations generally have fewer amenities and weather may not be as desirable. Some locations in rural communities are even offering free land to build a home, and some even offer tax incentives. You can search the term "free land" on the Internet or go to cfra.org, the Center For Rural Affairs, for more information.

3. Move in with your children or have them move in with you. Costs can be reduced significantly as you combine households. With the economic downturn resulting in higher unemployment and uncertainty, children are living with their parents longer. With the poor investment performance of their investment portfolios over the past decade combined with inflation, parents may even welcome their children back home to share living expenses.

4. Refinance your existing mortgage if prudent. If your cash flow is steady, such as from Social Security, government pensions, etc., you may consider extending your mortgage, thus reducing your monthly payment.

5. If you home's value has decreased in the past few years, determine if your property taxes are higher than they should be based upon your home's assessed value. If so, contest your home's assessed value with your local tax assessor's office. They should be able to help guide you through the process.

Entertainment and Recreation

As I mentioned at the beginning of this chapter, retirement is a lifestyle, not a destination, so complete Appendix C to define your retirement lifestyle and coordinate it with a new budget

(Appendix F). Since most people would like to do more things than they can comfortably afford, here are some unique tips that may help you accomplish more with the same money.

1. If you are a member of AARP, show your card at local restaurants and movie theaters to see if they offer a discount.

2. Many community colleges sponsor day trips to local attractions for a low fee.

3. Senior/multigeneration centers are available in most local communities and many offer low cost exercise and art classes.

Other Expenses

There are many ways to reduce expenses on things you already buy. Here are a few ways you may benefit.

1. Use the convection setting when operating your oven (if it has that option).

2. Search for senior discounts on the Internet at sites such as sciddy.com or seniordiscounts.com.

3. When you buy a car, consider buying one with a standard transmission. Initially, they are cheaper and over the long run you will save money on gasoline, brakes, and transmission repairs as well. When buying that car, do so at the end of the month as quotas need to be met and better deals can be made.

4. For those taking classes at a university to learn about interesting subjects, consider renting or downloading electronic versions to save a few dollars. Sites such as Bookrenter.com, Chegg.com, Gutenberg.org, and Bartelby.org may help.

5. Purchase "forever" stamps from the post office in bulk so your postage costs will never increase.

6. Call international numbers from your phone for free by using freephone2phone.com. In exchange for listening to a short advertisement, you receive ten minutes of free talk time to landlines in more than fifty countries.

Section Six—How to Reduce Risk

As the saying goes, "The more things change, the more they stay the same." This may be true for some things in life but certainly not for the investment markets. During the past decade, we have endured two asset bubbles that led to two recessions, two anemic recoveries, and an uncertain future. Congratulations are in order since you have endured the worst decade to invest in stocks since such data began compilation in 1820 and still have some sanity and wealth left.

With yields on US treasury securities at/near all-time lows (as of January 31, 2012, the five-year treasury yield is 0.71 percent, the ten-year treasury yield is 1.80 percent, and the thirty-year treasury yield is 2.93 percent) and the prospect of large budget deficits as far as the eye can see, higher interest rates and inflation seem to be on the intermediate-term horizon. As interest rates increase, the principal value of a bond decreases. As the bond approaches its maturity date, the principal value will generally approach its face value. So if the US government can refinance its debt in the future, the face value of the bond will be paid, as well as any accrued interest, to the bond holder at maturity. Between when you purchased the bond and the maturity date, the market value of the bond can be higher or lower, depending upon interest rates and credit risk.

If US treasuries return less than they have for the past thirty years, where does one invest for income and relatively low amount of risk? Good question. The answer depends upon the income needed from your portfolio, your risk tolerance, how long you plan to need the income, and if you desire the income to grow over time (maybe with inflation, for example).

There are many ways to reduce risk in your portfolio, but all involve some type of opportunity cost. Unfortunately, the compliance/supervision department of the broker/dealer and investment adviser that I am currently affiliated with will not permit me to describe many of these risk reductions strategies or even mention them in a list format, so I will not discuss any of them as I do not want to provide an incomplete list to you. Such censorship is, in my opinion, completely unnecessary but part of what we as advisers must tolerate.

So what can you do to reduce portfolio risk? Good question. I wish I could explain them to you, but your best strategy may be to ask an adviser who is experienced in such methodologies and not just using diversification, market timing, relative strength, asset allocation, or insurance based investments. Ask yourself or your investment professional what is being done to protect not only the nominal value of your assets but the relative value. The art is how to combine the strategies without sacrificing too much upside potential. The "recipe" will depend upon your unique situation.

When you buy a new car for someone you love, you are concerned about safety features, such as seat belts, air bags, automated controls, etc. If a model was a few thousand dollars cheaper but lacked all the safety features (assuming no government regulations), would you buy it for that person? Sure, that money will be available to be spent/invested elsewhere, but if an accident occurs, you may not be able to enjoy that money with them because of severe injury or even death. The same holds true about your investments. Protect what you have.

Let me reiterate: I believe it is the avoidance of severe losses, not the ability to make big gains that is responsible for better performance over time.

CHAPTER EIGHT

▽

Retirement
Distribution Planning

*As in all successful ventures, the foundation
of a good retirement is planning.*
—Earl Nightingale

The shift from "selling your time" to "selling your investments" to live on can be a stressful one, especially if finances are tight or if the financial markets are volatile. Trying to determine what asset classes you should invest in now, when changes are warranted, or what specific investment vehicles make the most sense is difficult, especially given today's global trading environment. So where do you start? There are many online services available that can help you if you want to do it yourself, but as discussed in previous chapters, this can take a considerable amount of time, energy, knowledge, and understanding and will probably take your focus off what you should be doing: enjoying retirement.

I strongly believe in designing retirement income plans with a "bucket" approach. What is a bucket approach and what are the potential benefits? A bucket approach can be visualized by simply dividing your investable retirement assets (this does not include your emergency fund) into three buckets: one for short-term income needs (one to three years); one for intermediate-term income and spending needs (years four through ten); and one for long-term income and spending needs (years eleven-plus). When the short-term bucket is emptied, the intermediate-term bucket is used to refill it, and the long-term bucket is used to refill the intermediate-term bucket. For those who are greatly concerned about longevity risk there is a fourth bucket, the extra-long-term bucket.

With careful and diligent planning, investing, and monitoring, this process will help reduce the possibility of running out of money before you run out of time.

Many investment strategies can be used to manage the money in the buckets. My main strategy is the prudent use of risk management. In the bucket approach, do not let a hole develop in the bottom of any bucket or it will seriously jeopardize the overall strategy. It is important to preserve the integrity of the buckets and maintain them as well as possible by using investments and products that utilize various risk management methodologies. Each risk management methodology has its own unique set of advantages and disadvantages, so develop a tailored, prudent solution based on your own needs and goals.

Many retirement income plans are based on a static investment return that occurs every year, such as an average portfolio return of 7 percent. As you know, this just won't occur every year, so I would regard those income plans as being worth less than the cost of the paper and ink to print it.

How do you plan for something when you have no idea what will happen? In basic terms, what I do for clients is the following:

1. Begin by determining your retirement income needs (there is that dreaded budget again!).

2. Determine your guaranteed sources of retirement

income (pensions, social security, annuities, etc.) and if they include cost of living adjustments (COLAs).

3. Determine if you would like to handle potential long-term care expenses out of pocket or transfer that risk to an insurance company. If you want to assume the risk, how much "coverage" do you want? Subtract that from your retirement distribution plan assets.

4. Determine how much you would like to set aside as an emergency fund. Subtract that from your retirement distribution plan assets.

5. Determine if you are concerned about longevity risk and plan accordingly.

6. What inflation rate would you assume for your expenses?

7. What would be your expected withdrawal rate?

8. Determine and implement your investment plan.

9. Create a spreadsheet, and "run" your model.

10. Review, monitor, and make appropriate changes to steps one through nine at least annually.

Again, I believe it is the avoidance of severe losses, not the ability to make big gains that is responsible for better performance over time.

CHAPTER NINE

Health Care

Father Time is not always a hard parent, and, though he tarries
for none of his children, often lays his hand lightly upon those
who have used him well; making them old men and women
inexorably enough, but leaving their hearts and spirits young and
in full vigor. With such people the gray head is but the impression
of the old fellow's hand in giving them his blessing, and every
wrinkle but a notch in the quiet calendar of a well-spent life.
Taking care of oneself with proper diet and exercise over the
course of a lifetime is no guarantee to a long, healthy life, nor
should it be considered a burden for life is too precious to waste.
—Charles Dickens

Section One—Health Wellness Plan

Before beginning any health/exercise routine, please consult a qualified physician. As part of your overall financial wellness plan, I also encourage you to develop a health wellness plan. Sure, the cost of eating higher quality food, using a gym membership, and working with a health professional to monitor your plan will alter your budget, but how much more can you enjoy what life has to offer when you feel better, have more energy, and live longer? The cost of health care should be reduced as you cleanse the toxins out of your body over time. Even consider such things as purchasing a better bed to improve the quality of sleep and/or better shoes to make walking and exercise less demanding on your body. You get the idea.

Beloved, I wish above all things that you may prosper and be in health, even as your soul prospers (3 John 1:2, NKJV).

Section Two—Safety Net

The cost of health care increases the lack of access to quality health care. What do I mean by that? Simply put, as the cost of health care increases, those who are wealthy or have health insurance that pays doctors what they want and will accept will have access to quality health care. For those who do not, they will have to stand in line for care at a facility that will accept lower reimbursements. As demand for health care increases with the aging of the baby boomers, this dichotomy will become more and more apparent. Medicare and Medicaid are essentially bankrupt right now (see the Medicare and Medicaid Trustees' latest reports at www.ssa.gov/oact/tr/2012/index.html and www.cms.gov/ReportsTrustFunds), and entitlement reform always seems to be on the horizon.

So how do you prepare for this eventual reality of "self-insurance"? First by trying to create healthy habits by developing and sticking to a health and wellness plan as described above. Second by understanding that health-care coverage should be a goal you want to achieve in your financial plan. Third by having your children become doctors. Hopefully you can achieve all three, but for most of us, if we adequately address the first two, that will be enough.

Since 1981, the inflation rate for medical care has increased more than the overall inflation rate for all items each year. It has done so in fifty-nine of the seventy-three years from 1936 to 2008, according to the Bureau of Labor Statistics. Depending upon your age, overall health, and plan for longevity, costs will be much higher when you retire and probably need more medical care. Consequently, part of your retirement budget must include a realistic estimate of these costs. Transferring risk to insurance companies is a good start, but there are costs those policies do not cover.

Section Three—Long-Term Care

This is probably the most unpleasant need of insurance for most people. Being unable to care for oneself is a humbling thought and not a pretty mental picture. If this, however, is part of your future, at least be able to afford the best care possible and hopefully leave an inheritance for those you love and respect.

For an informative guide on what to consider before purchasing a long-term care policy, I recommend visiting www.naic.org and downloading their "Shopper's Guide to Long-Term Care Insurance." The National Association of Insurance Commissioners (NAIC) was formed in 1871 and its members consist of the chief insurance regulators in all fifty states, the District of Columbia, and five US territories. Its main purpose is to protect the interests of insurance consumers by providing guidelines for regulations for state's use and education.

Long-term care insurance is complicated and there are many different types with different features and benefits. I strongly suggest you read the NAIC guide mentioned above before meeting with a qualified, experienced adviser.

Section Four—Support Groups

At some point in our lives, we will need the help of others to help us cope with accidents, injuries, sickness, and death. Local support groups or Internet blogs and chat sessions can ease our burdens and brighten our outlook. I encourage you to develop relationships with various local support groups and even volunteer to help those in need.

CHAPTER TEN

▽

Legacy

The legacy we leave is part of the ongoing foundations of life. Those who came before leave us the world we live in. Those who will come after will have only what we leave them. We are stewards of this world, and we have a calling on our lives to leave it better than how we found it, even if it seems like such a small part.
—Jim Rohn

Now that you have successfully navigated the waters from conception to the present day, the questions I ask you are, "What do you want your legacy to be?" and "How many people did you help and how do you want them to remember you?" These are powerful questions, and many will not want to address them, but everyone should. So how do we begin? First by understanding that giving money to a charity or to a family member or a friend after we are dead is not what I am talking about. Rather, I am referring to the stewardship of our time and money over the course of our lifetime.

Section One—
Considerations, Understanding of Needs

Most everyone has heard the proverb, "Give a man a fish and you feed him for a day. Teach a man to fish and you feed him for a lifetime." You can apply the same wisdom to your legacy planning. Everyone has heard of the lottery winners who eventually declare bankruptcy. Provided with the opportunity to make a difference in their lives and many others, impulsive spending, poor investment decisions, etc., left them with nothing but regret and thoughts of what could have been. Obviously, they were not prepared for the windfall they received.

So how do you divide your estate so everyone agrees or at least understands the rationale?

First you must introduce your family members to the concept. Calling each member personally to determine when they are available to meet is a good start, possibly during the holidays or schedule a family reunion; whatever makes the most sense. If you are uncomfortable doing so, choose one child you feel has the best overall relationship with the entire family and let him or her take the lead on this step. Let them all know it has been a goal of yours for the entire family to get together for fellowship and that is it not because you are terminally ill. You don't want the rumor mill to go wild.

Second, make sure the discussion is more about personal values and future goals than about money and things. Cherish this time to get to know more about each other and let them know why you are making this a priority at this particular time.

Third, after the discussions are over, enjoy the time together with fun activities, having an old-fashioned family dinner, watching an old movie, etc. This will take the focus off inheritance and on to joyous endeavors.

Only by getting to know what is important to each member

of your family can you begin to determine how to divide up your assets.

Remember, an equal share is not always equitable. For example, if you have a farm and only one of your three children wants to stay and commit his or her life to running it, why divide the deed three ways when only one is doing all the work? What if you have a child with special needs? Or if one child has sacrificed his or her career to help take care of you?

By having the conversation now, you can build a sound legacy plan with reduced familial conflict, rather than doing so during a difficult and emotional time in the future.

Section Two— The Four Cornerstones of Legacy Planning

Values are intangible and rarely discussed. Since they are not "physical property," how do you preserve them and ultimately share them for generations to come? It may not be easy, but take a few moments to reflect upon your parents' "code of conduct" and what "made or makes them tick." Many of their values have become your values even though you may not have noticed until now. Photographs, handwritten letters/notes, greeting cards, and special recipes are some examples and, with some work (albums, scrapbooks, etc.), can be preserved and shared with many future generations. If possible, have the children and grandchildren help you create this portion of your legacy a few weekends each summer.

Personal possessions are tangible, and because of their sentimental value, they are difficult to divide equally. Therefore, it is important to ask each family member to list their favorite items and write down why each item is so special to them. Family heirlooms can and will vary dramatically in notional value, thus creating another potential for conflict, so consider this as part of the overall legacy plan. Now that you have the lists in front of you, compare them and if two or more members list the same item, by all means have a spirited conversation, but reinforce that family and values are more important than possessions. Bottom line here is that you have collected many possessions during your life and by discussing what is important to each member of your family, you have the ability to make the decisions as to how you feel it is best to distribute your estate. By doing so now, you can hopefully prevent future conflict. Not everyone will agree, but they should respect your decisions.

Financial assets can be tangible or intangible. Intangible items, such as stocks, bonds, checking accounts, and IRA accounts are easy to divide and most do not have an emotional tie to them. Create transfer on death (TOD) accounts with your investment adviser, payable on death (POD) accounts at your local banking institution, or place such assets into your trust for disbursement. By doing so, you will avoid probate for these items. Tangible financial assets such as real estate, precious stones/metals, artwork, and classic automobiles may have sentimental value, so treat them accordingly, as in the previous section.

How to deal with final wishes and instructions is not a topic most families openly discuss very often. Just the idea that life ends for all of us is not a pleasant thought. Having to face the eventuality and making sure your wishes are carried out, however, is worth the effort. Doing so will help you define your legacy, and the discussions with your children can ease their emotions when the time comes. Begin by writing down (or creating a spreadsheet) how you want your estate to be distributed and any final wishes and instructions you want fulfilled. Then meet with a qualified professional to set up a will/trust. Don't forget to fund the trust if that is the method you determine is most prudent.

Section Three—
Be a Blessing to Others for Its Own Sake

How many times during your life would you have liked to have received a helping hand? Not one where you felt a sense of entitlement but one where you felt a sincere thank you for helping you get out of a tough spot. Generosity can take many forms, not only financially. Spending time with friends and family to help them cope with life's many challenges, volunteering at a local support group or your church, or coaching a youth sports team are a few examples where you can make a positive difference in someone's life and own a sense of accomplishment and satisfaction in your own. I encourage you to get out of your comfort zone a little and think about how your individual talents and gifts can be used to bless others without expecting anything in return. I am sure the world would be a better place.

Personally, members of my family have volunteered by teaching Sunday school at our local church for more than a decade, coached youth basketball, and united divided families using faith as a cornerstone. In my financial services practice, one of my goals is to provide pro bono services a few hours each week to disabled veterans and their family. My father was a lifetime member of the Disabled American Veterans, and before he died, we discussed how I could be a blessing to so many who have fought for our freedom. Freedom is not free, but at least my services to those who fought for our freedom can be.

Many of you may be talented at teaching and bright in subjects that many students have difficulty learning. Volunteering a couple hours per week at your local school may improve their chances of graduating and have the extra benefit of knowing that someone cares. Some of you may be talented at art and can volunteer at local community centers to encourage a child's development of his or her creative abilities. Positive reinforcement of a job well done is vital to fending off the negativity in society today. You can think of many more examples and how you can be a blessing to others. You just have to get out and do it. Congratulations to those of you who do so.

Section Four—Estate Planning Considerations

Not being an estate-planning attorney, I am not qualified to discuss all the details of wills, trusts, conservatorships, etc. After years of dealing with clients, however, I have developed the following estate-planning checklist you may find helpful.

1. Have a last will and testament. Make sure to have a "pour-over provision" and if you have young children, a section naming guardian(s).

2. Consider a living trust. If you (and your attorney) decide this is the prudent choice, make sure you transfer assets into the trust so they avoid the cost and time-consuming process of probate.

3. Take care of health-care directives by creating a living will and a durable power of attorney for health care. If you are unable to make medical decisions for yourself because of injury or other form of incapacity, this can provide the authority for someone you choose to make them for you.

4. Similar to the item above, create a durable power of attorney for your financial assets. Choose a person you trust who is capable of making knowledgeable financial decisions. This person is known as the "attorney in fact."

5. Make sure all beneficiary forms are updated with correct information. This includes IRA accounts, your company-sponsored retirement plans, insurance policies, bank accounts, brokerage accounts, and

many others. In some states, if you own your home you can even file a transfer-on-death (TOD) deed, so your home avoids probate. Try to have most of your financial assets in TOD form (banks usually use payable-on-death terminology).

6. If you decide to leave an inheritance for minor children, you should consider creating a custodianship for those assets. If you do not designate a custodian, the probate court will do it for you, and they may appoint someone you wouldn't have. To prevent this from happening, include a custodianship in your will or trust.

7. If your estate is near the estate tax threshold (including life insurance proceeds if not owned by an irrevocable life insurance trust), consider meeting with an estate-planning attorney. Estate tax law changes occur frequently, so review your plan annually.

8. Do an insurance needs analysis every few years or if your life situation changes (marriage/divorce, new child, home purchase, etc.). Make sure to include disability, life, health, and property and casualty (such as liability, homeowners, automobile, earthquake, flood, etc.).

9. If you own a business, create a business continuation plan.

10. Create a legacy plan that includes final wishes and instructions.

11. Store your documents in a safe, secure, and readily accessible place.

Section Five—Inheritance of IRA Accounts

When an account holder dies, what becomes of their retirement plan assets? The answer depends upon the type of retirement plan and beneficiary designations. Since laws serving the financial services industry frequently change, the following is based upon federal law at the time this book was published and is not intended to be tax or legal advice, so please seek personalized advice from a qualified tax professional.

Traditional IRA Accounts

When a traditional IRA account owner dies and you are the surviving spouse, you have basically four choices: roll the account over into the surviving spouse's own retirement account, elect to continue to treat the account as the deceased spouse's account, use the account to fund the A or B trust established in the deceased spouse's estate plan, or take a complete distribution. Let's briefly discuss each of these.

1. Most opt for rolling the deceased spouse's IRA into their own retirement account. All of the deferred income taxes associate with the IRA account will continue to be deferred until a distribution (withdrawal) occurs. The surviving spouse will be able to use his or her age for determining required minimum distributions (RMD) that must begin by the April 15 of the following year when they turn seventy and a half. For example, if you are seventy and a half on July 1, you may delay taking an RMD until April 15 of the following year. Keep in mind, however, that if you do this, two RMDs must be taken during the same year (last year's and this year's), so you may be kicked up to the next income tax bracket.

2. If the first spouse dies between the ages of fifty-nine and a half and seventy and a half and the surviving spouse is younger than age fifty-nine and a half, you may wish to continue to treat the IRA as the deceased spouse's account. In this instance, the surviving spouse will have the ability to take withdrawals from the account without incurring the 10 percent early withdrawal penalty. The IRA will continue to be tax deferred if no withdrawals are taken. Once the surviving spouse turns fifty-nine and a half, you can roll it into your IRA account.

3. If the IRA becomes a part of the deceased spouse's A or B trust, the surviving spouse will be required to start taking minimum distributions calculated over their life expectancy and will not be able to change the beneficiaries of the account.

4. Finally, the surviving spouse can elect to have the proceeds of the IRA sent to them. Since this is a distribution, you will owe ordinary income taxes on the total amount.

When a Traditional IRA account owner dies and you are not the surviving spouse, you have two choices: an Inherited IRA or cashing out the account. Let's briefly discuss both options.

1. If you decide to transfer the account into an inherited IRA, IRS regulations require that payments to a beneficiary begin no later than December 31 following the year of death and continue over the beneficiary's lifetime (you can take withdrawals when needed, but the amount withdrawn will be included in your taxable income). This is what is known in the industry as a stretch IRA. The objective is to stretch the beneficiary's payments over a lengthy period of time in order to

possibly obtain more favorable tax and economic results. If there were more than one beneficiary for the account, the IRS uses the older beneficiary's age to calculate the amount of the payments. If there is a significant age difference between beneficiaries, you may wish to split the inherited IRA into multiple IRAs. You have until December 31 of the year following the account owner's death to do so. Factors to consider when stretching an IRA include possible changes to the tax laws, inflation, currency fluctuations, and other risks.

2. You can cash out the account in full. The entire amount will be included in your taxable income in the year of the distribution, so you may wish to have taxes withheld. No early penalties are assessed, however.

ROTH IRA Accounts

When a Roth IRA owner dies and you are the surviving spouse and sole beneficiary, you can choose to either treat the Roth IRA as your own (this includes rolling it into your existing Roth IRA if you have one) or delay distributions until the decedent would have reached age seventy and a half. If you don't treat the Roth IRA as your own, the RMD rules that apply to traditional IRAs as described above will apply to the Roth IRA. That is why most elect the first option.

When a Roth IRA owner dies and you are not the surviving spouse, you can choose to distribute the entire account by the end of the fifth calendar year after the year of the decedent's death or choose to accept payments over your life expectancy and must begin before the end of the calendar year following the year of the decedent's death. If the decedent had more than one Roth IRA account, the beneficiary can combine all such interests they are due into one inherited Roth IRA account.

Pretty simple so far, but now we have to talk about the potential for income taxes. Most investors think that when you invest in or convert a traditional IRA, 401(k), or 403b to a Roth IRA, you have already paid the tax on the amount contributed or converted, that the account grows tax deferred, and any distributions are tax and penalty free. That is just not true. Let's discuss how Roth IRAs are not tax and penalty free vehicles and include an example.

First, let us define "qualified distribution." A qualified distribution is any withdrawal from your Roth IRA that is:

1. Made after the five-year waiting period, which begins on the first day of the year when a conversion was made or the first day of the year for which a contribution was made. For example, if you contributed $3,000 to your Roth IRA on April 15, 2010, for tax year 2009, your five-year waiting period for this contribution would end on December 31, 2013. If you converted $2,000 on the same date, the five-year waiting period for this conversion would end on December 31, 2014.

2. Or

   - made on or after the date you reach age fifty-nine and a half
   - used to purchase or rebuild a first home ($10,000 limit)
   - made because of your disability
   - made payable to a designated beneficiary or to your estate after your death

Such "qualified distributions" are not subject to income or the additional 10 percent penalty tax.

A "nonqualified distribution" is any distribution that is not a qualified distribution. All nonqualified distributions are subjected to the additional 10 percent penalty tax on the taxable part of the distribution, except for the following situations:

- You have reached age fifty-nine and a half.

- You are disabled.

- You are the designated beneficiary of a deceased IRA owner.

- You use the distribution to pay certain qualified first-time homebuyer amounts.

- You have elected to take distributions over your life expectancy

- Your family's unreimbursed medical expenses are greater than 7.5 percent of your adjusted gross income.

- You are paying medical insurance premiums after losing your job.

- The distributions are not more than your qualified higher education expenses.

- The distribution is due to an IRS levy of the qualified plan.

- The distribution is a qualified reservist distribution.

Now that we have the "qualification" matters under control, let us assume the owner of a Roth IRA dies before the end of the five-year period beginning with the first taxable year for which a contribution was made to a Roth IRA set up for the owner's benefit, or the five-year period starting with the year of a conversion contribution from a traditional IRA or a rollover from a qualified retirement plan to the Roth IRA. In each case, the distribution is not qualified and is includible in the beneficiary's gross income in the same manner as it would have been included in the owner's income had it been distributed to the IRA owner when he or she was alive. Consequently, both income and the penalty tax may apply. Tax laws are complex and change frequently, so please discuss your situation with a qualified tax specialist.

For example, John Smith, a widower, died in February 2011 and left his two beneficiaries with equal shares. The account value on the date of death was $60,000 and contained regular contributions of $20,000, a 2007 conversion of $10,000, and earnings of $30,000. Each beneficiary will receive equal shares of each component, namely $10,000 of regular contributions, $5,000 of conversion contributions, and $15,000 of earnings. Since the distributions are made before the end of the five year waiting period to be classified as a qualified distribution, each beneficiary will have to include $15,000 in their gross income for 2011. The 10 percent additional penalty tax does not apply in this case because the distribution was a result of the death of the account owner.

Another example is Bob Smith, who died in February 2011 at age fifty-five and named his wife, Mary, age fifty, as the sole beneficiary. The account value on the date of death was $50,000. Bob opened the Roth IRA account in April 2008, contributed $5,000 each for tax years 2007, 2008, and 2009, and converted his $20,000 traditional IRA to this Roth IRA in 2010. They have not yet paid income tax on the conversion in 2010 as they decided to use the special two-year rule to include half of the converted amount as income in tax years 2011 and 2012. Mary has two options; she can either continue the Roth IRA as her own or delay distributions until 2026 when Bob would be seventy and a half. Mary chooses to continue the Roth IRA as her own and will include $10,000 in her gross income for tax years 2011 and 2012. No other income tax or penalty tax is owed unless she takes a distribution from the Roth IRA before the five-year waiting period is completed.

CHAPTER ELEVEN

▽

Compensation

Price is what you pay. Value is what you get.
—Warren Buffett

There are three ways you can pay someone for their financial advice: fee only, fee-based, or commission. Each has its place, and how you pay for the advice should depend upon your needs and goals, not your adviser's.

Always remember, bad advice is costly no matter what the price.

Make sure your adviser provides you with ADV Part 2B (also known as the "brochure supplement" which includes information about the specific individuals, acting on behalf of the investment adviser, who actually provide the investment advice and interact with the client) that has been filed with the Financial Institutional Regulatory Authority (FINRA). You can look up your advisers' history at www.finra.org/brokercheck. Also, be sure your investment adviser provides you with a performance report at least annually. Comparison to appropriate benchmarks and/or indexes should be part of the annual review.

Before we tackle the question of how to pay someone for their financial advice, let's briefly explain each methodology.

Section One—Compensation Structures

Fee Only

Fee-only planners charge by the hour or have a set fee for financial advice, and as a result, they are a fiduciary. They receive their compensation directly from their clients. Fee-only planners can be asset-based, flat fee, hourly, or net worth and income.

Asset-based planners are the most common type of compensation plan. The main advantage touted by both planners and clients is that the fee is based upon the amount of assets managed, so there is a built in incentive to increase client returns. Some disadvantages are mainly conflicts of interest that many advisers do not discuss with their clients, such as the temptation to take risks that are not prudent given the client's needs and goals or to discourage taking assets out of the account to spend/ invest elsewhere.

Flat-fee planners provide service for a fee. Some provide investment advice and implementation into "no-load" products (all products have a cost, so please make sure to ask your adviser), while others refer you to an investment professional. They do not charge a fee based upon the amount of assets you have, the products you buy, or earn a fee for referring you to someone else. They provide a service for a fee, plain and simple.

Hourly fee planners/advisers charge—you guessed it—by the hour for advice. It may be a good starting point to see whether you and the planner/adviser are compatible.

Net worth and income, in my opinion, offers the least conflicts of interest but require a planner/adviser who has a broad base of knowledge and experience in many different types of assets, such as artwork, collectibles, and real estate. Because fees are based upon some combination of net worth and income, there is no incentive to dissuade a client from selling one type of asset to acquire another if it makes financial sense. This may also be appropriate for those clients who have a majority of their net worth tied up in their business or company-based retirement plans.

Commission

Commission-based advisers receive their compensation from the product sponsor (when using a packaged product, such as a mutual fund, unit investment trust, insurance, annuity, etc.) or their broker/dealer (for trades in individual securities, such as stocks, bonds, exchange traded funds, etc.) when a transaction (buy/sell) occurs. Commission-based advisers can also receive trail commissions, known as section 12b-1 fees. Trades must meet suitability requirements only at the time of the trade, so be sure to monitor your portfolio and communicate with your broker regularly. Commission-based advisers are not fiduciaries.

Fee Based

Fee-based advisers are a hybrid of the fee-only and commission based adviser. They are licensed to provide both services and have the responsibility to disclose any and all conflicts of interest.

Section Two—How to Decide Which Is Better for You

Every adviser should have an area of expertise and develop his or her business plan accordingly. Since there are so many more complexities and regulations in the financial markets now than in the recent past, it is nearly impossible for one adviser to be fully versed in all aspects of financial planning, investment management, heritage planning, estate planning, insurance, tax accounting, and economics. Consequently, you will be better served by having multiple advisers who are experts in their chosen professions and have the abilities to work as part of a team on your behalf.

Let me provide an example. You have a portfolio of $5,000,000 and need an after-tax, inflation-adjusted income of $120,000 per year for the next twenty years. Your major concerns are that you do not run out of money and that you have the ability to leave an inheritance to your family and local charities. How much risk do you need to take, what should you invest in, and how should your investment adviser be compensated? Based on these assumptions, you can afford to be conservative if you want to be. The certainty of meeting your income goal is high as long as you don't lose principal to either market loss or inflation.

For someone in this situation, it may be better just to buy a laddered portfolio of individual bonds (e.g., municipal, I-bonds, US treasury, foreign I-bonds) using a commission-based broker. If you decide you would like to have your account actively managed, it may be better to have a portion of your account be commission based (the bond ladder for the income goal) and a fee-based account using exchange traded funds, mutual funds, and individual equities for the actively managed portion you would like to see grow to provide the inheritance.

A fee-only planner will usually recommend a portfolio of index mutual funds using a strategic asset allocation model using a systematic withdrawal plan for your income needs. Alternatively, you could have three separate advisers, one fee-only to determine your risk tolerance, insurance needs, and your income and inheritance plans; a commission-based broker experienced with building laddered bond strategies to meet your income goal; and a fee-based adviser to manage the assets for your inheritance goal. You should also consider a tax adviser as part of your team to make sure to mitigate taxes as much as possible and an estate-planning attorney to make sure your assets are protected from unforeseen events and reduce estate taxes as much as possible. An insurance agent may also be needed to transfer risk from you and your estate to an insurance company. You see, it all depends on how much uncertainty you want to eliminate.

I could provide many examples, but I hope you get the idea

that reducing uncertainty means you need to go through the exercises mentioned throughout this book and determine what needs to be done, and by whom, for you to feel comfortable with your financial situation.

$\triangledown$

Putting It All Together

*It's not hard to make decisions when you
know what your values are.*
—Walt Disney

I hope you have learned a little from reading this book. Now comes the difficult part—actually following through on getting your financial health diagnosed (where you are today), developing a game-plan for improvement (how you get to your destination), and making changes when necessary (navigating detours). This is the third "p"—practice.

The worksheets in the appendixes should be a starting point for understanding your current financial situation and beginning the process of developing a team of advisers who will work in your best interest. You may wish (and I encourage you to do so) to add additional questions or worksheet items to conform more to your individual situation and needs. Do not get bogged down in minutiae, however, as that is usually counterproductive.

Make sure to understand the personal biases in Section Two of Chapter One, and when you make a financial decision, go through the exercise of how those biases were affecting you initially, and then after you have considered their affect. Keep those analyses in a notebook for future reference, to determine whether you clearly thought through each decision. This will help you perfect your decision-making process, or, at worst, at least remember why you decided to do what you did.

Designing your lifestyle is probably the most difficult task presented in this book because it involves not only yourself but many others. Breaking down the task from the big picture to distinct goals is time consuming and requires a lot of introspection. Different aspects of your life, such as work, family, health, finances, faith, friendships, and recreation will all need to be addressed not only separately but together. Consider it your own personal recipe for your life and you want every day to be a vacation and every meal to be a banquet.

As mentioned earlier, retirement should be a chapter of your life where you are able to do those things you always wanted to but didn't have the time. What you decide to retire to can be a great motivator, so make sure and define this as soon as you can.

Understand and implement risk-management strategies you believe can help you achieve your goals. Do not let the financial markets be the sole determinant of your financial future.

Determining your legacy is also difficult for many but should be coordinated with your lifestyle plan. Deepening relationships with family and friends is truly priceless.

Diversification does not guarantee success but can help manage risk and reduce the chance of failure.

Divide your portion to seven, or even to eight, for you do not know what misfortune may occur on the earth (Ecclesiastes 11:2).

When you open an investment account, make sure the institution that has custodial responsibilities is legitimate. Do your due diligence. Writing a check to the personal name of your broker, insurance agent, or banker should send up warning signals. Be careful. As President Reagan said, "Trust, but verify."

There are many financial planning programs available to help you draft a plan. Most free services are limited in scope and do not provide the oversight of an experienced, knowledgeable financial planner/adviser. After carefully researching many planning programs for my business, I decided on one that was easy for my clients to understand, had a lot of visual aids (since most people are visually oriented), and provided me with the level of detail necessary to adequately analyze their situation. If you decide to pursue the do-it-yourself route, make sure to run multiple scenarios using carefully thought through "what-if" analysis, which is extremely important as changes in tax rates, interest rates, inflation, sequence of returns, etc. can cause meaningful deviations in your plan.

As I wrote in Chapter Two, "If you are a specialist in behavioral finance, investments, insurance, taxes, and estate planning, then you can truly do it yourself, assuming you have the time. Otherwise, it is probably better to assemble a team of professionals who will work on your behalf to develop and implement a holistic financial plan."

I am not saying this to be self-serving. Rather, I am recommending that you rely on the expertise of others. This is similar to hiring an electrician, plumber, carpenter, attorney, mechanic, et. al. This is dissimilar because you must disclose your assets, liabilities, income, goals, etc., and these are very personal. It is just this reason why many people do not hire a financial adviser. Get over it! All registered advisers must comply with a code of ethics that includes not only privacy protection but disclosure of conflicts of interest. They work on your behalf and have fiduciary responsibility to do so. Not all financial advisers, financial planners, investment advisers, etc. are created equal, however. Some are technical, others more fundamental. Some are educated by books while others have decades of experience. Be careful who you select as your adviser and make sure he or she is experienced in those areas you need help with. For those with a complex situation, you may wish to use the services of multiple advisers (financial planner, investment adviser, insurance agent, estate planning attorney, and accountant) and have them work with each other; the cost will be higher, but it may create a better overall outcome.

Plans fail for lack of counsel, but with many advisers they succeed (Proverbs 15:22 NIV).

If you decide to hire a team of advisers, remember that you are the customer and hub of the wheel, they are the spokes, and the overall plan is the rubber that meets the road. If you do not feel you have the expertise to be the hub of the wheel, you need to designate one professional who has a basic understanding of each of the spokes of the wheel and have him or her lead the team.

From everyone who has been given much, much will be demanded; and from the one who has been entrusted with much, much more will be asked (Luke 12:48, NIV).

It is extremely important to understand the difference between information and advice. Information is factual data; advice is a recommendation offered as a guide to action. Information is not a hot stock tip or something you read on a blog; rather, it is something factual. So to turn what you read or hear into information, you must go through the process of determining whether it is true or false. Advice is provided from someone and can be either good or bad, depending upon the source and/or the amount of information used.

Bad advice, no matter how inexpensive, is costly.

One last quote that may be apropos: *I can't change the fact that my paintings don't sell. But the time will come when people will recognize that they are worth more than the value of the paints used in the picture* (Vincent van Gogh).

I know the time will come when people will recognize that

the words on the pages of this book are worth many times what was paid, but only if it inspires them to take action.

End of the book; the beginning of your future.

Appendix A—
Questions to Ask a Financial Adviser

Adviser Information

Name: _____

Business Name, if different: _____

Address: _____

City: _____ State: _____ Zip: _____

Phone:_____

About Your Practice

1. How many clients do you currently serve?

    ___ Fewer than 25   ___ 25–50

    ___ 51–100   ___ More than 100

2. What are your clients' most common investment objectives? Please rank in order, with 1 being most common and 4 least common.

    1) _____   3) _____

    2) _____   4) _____

3. What is your clients' most common age range? Please rank in order on a scale from 1 to 4, with 1 being most common and 4 least common.

    ___ Under 35   ___ 36–50   ___ 51–65   ___ Over 65

4. What is your clients' most common income range? (Total income per household before taxes.) Please rank in order from 1 to 4 with 1 being most common and 4 least common

___ < $50,000 yr.   ___ $50,001–$100,000 yr.

___ $100,001–$150,000 yr   ___ > $150,000 yr.

5. Can you take discretionary authority over client accounts?

___ Yes   ___ No

6. Who is the custodian of client accounts? _____

_____

7. Will you provide me with references from clients? ___ Yes ___ No

a. Name: _____ Phone: _____

b. Name: _____ Phone: _____

c. Name: _____ Phone: _____

8. Will you provide me with a sample copy of a financial plan or investment plan recommendations?   ___ Yes   ___ No

9. Please provide me with a current copy of your form ADV, Part II, or disclosure document.

10. Do you have a succession plan?   ___ Yes   ___ No

If yes, please provide a brief description: _____

_____

_____

11. What is your company's mission statement? _____

_____

_____

Experience, Registrations, Education

1. How long have you been offering financial planning or investment advisory services? _____

2. How long have you been registered as an investment adviser or investment adviser representative? _____

3. What securities registrations, insurance licenses, and/or professional designations are you eligible to use?
   a. _____/ Yr. Received: _____
   b. _____/ Yr. Received: _____
   c. _____/ Yr. Received: _____
   d. _____/ Yr. Received: _____
   e. _____/ Yr. Received: _____
   f. _____/ Yr. Received: _____

4. What educational degrees have you earned?
   a. School: _____ Degree___ Major _____ Yr. ___
   b. School: _____ Degree___ Major _____ Yr. ___
   c. School: _____ Degree___ Major _____ Yr. ___

Services and Products

1. Which Financial Services do you provide? Please check all that apply.
   ___ Comprehensive Financial Plans
   ___ Investment and Asset Management
   ___ 401(k) Investment Advisory
   ___ Retirement Planning
   ___ Insurance
   ___ Brokerage Services
   ___ Mutual Fund Selection
   ___ Timing Services
   ___ Securities Research
   ___ Portfolio Monitoring
   ___ Tax Planning
   ___ Estate Planning
   ___ Tax Preparation
   ___ Business Planning

2. Will you provide a written analysis of my particular financial situation and recommendations? ___ Yes ___ No

3. Will you offer continuous advice? ___ Yes ___ No

4. Do you recommend specific investment products? ___ Yes ___ No

   ___ Stocks   ___ US Government Securities
   ___ Municipal Securities   ___ Corporate Bonds
   ___ Mutual Funds   ___ Exchange Traded Funds/Notes
   ___ Preferred Stocks   ___ Futures/Commodities
   ___ Insurance Products   ___ Limited Partnerships
   ___ Certificates of Deposit   ___ Unlisted REITs
   ___ Other (specify) _____

5. Do you provide assistance with implementation? ___ Yes ___ No

6. Briefly describe how you manage risk for clients: _____

   _____
   _____
   _____

7. Briefly describe how you determine which investments to buy:

   _____
   _____
   _____
   _____

8. Briefly describe how you determine when to buy or sell:

   _____
   _____
   _____
   _____
   _____

9. Briefly describe your financial planning process:

   _____
   _____
   _____
   _____
   _____

Compensation

1. How are you compensated? Please check all that apply.

___ Fee (specify):

___ Initial

___ Hourly

___ Retainer

___ Percentage of assets managed

___ Performance Fee

___ Commissions (specify):

___ Commissions and loads for financial products purchased or sold

___ Ongoing fees paid as commissions for financial products purchased

___ Fee offset (You charge a flat fee that is offset by commissions earned)

___ Salary

___ Other (specify) _____

2. How is your compensation calculated? Please indicate all that apply.

Based on an hourly rate of $ _____

Fee range of $ _____ to $ _____

Minimum fee of $ _____

Percentage of Assets _____ percent to _____ percent

Other (specify) _____

3. Are your fees negotiable? ___ Yes ___ No

4. Do you or any related party receive compensation from any persons or firms to whom I may be referred? ___ Yes ___ No

Regulatory and Compliance

If your answer to any of the following is yes, please complete the section describing the event or proceeding. (Attach a separate piece of paper if necessary.)

1. Has any court ever entered a judgment against you in connection with any investment related activity? ___ Yes ___ No

2. Have you ever been involved in an arbitration proceeding that was settled or decided against you? ___ Yes ___ No

3. Have you ever been the subject of an order issued by a:
   a. Federal regulatory agency? ___ Yes ___ No
   b. State regulatory agency? ___ Yes ___ No
   c. Self-regulatory agency? ___ Yes ___ No

4. Have you been discharged or permitted to resign because you were accused of violating industry standards or investment related statutes? ___ Yes ___ No

5. Are you currently involved, directly, or indirectly, in any regulatory investigation or action, customer complaint, civil litigation, or criminal proceeding? ___ Yes ___ No
   Description of event or proceeding:

   _____

   _____

   _____

   _____

   _____

Appendix B—Time Budget Worksheet and Instructions

To examine your current time allocation to varying tasks, fill out the time budget sheet with your current habits, beginning this week. Fill out another sheet with how you would like to allocate your time. Compare the two and determine how you can accomplish the transformation of your endeavors. This can be done on a weekly basis, if you prefer, to track time planned and spent.

Time Budget Worksheet

Task	Sun	Mon	Tues	Wed	Thu	Fri	Sat	Sun	Hours/ Week
Sleeping									
Working									
Commuting									
Exercise									
Meals									
Entertainment & Recreation									
Personal Hygiene									
Family Time									
Household Chores									
Television									
Social Networking									
Other									
Total									

Task	Sun	Mon	Tues	Wed	Thu	Fri	Sat	Sun	Hours/ Week
Hours Available	24	24	24	24	24	24	24	24	168
Total (from above)									
Hours Remaining									

Tips That May Help Keep You on Budget

1. Expect success in this exercise.

2. Avoid procrastination—begin and stick with it.

3. Prioritize your goals and try to "evolve" to meet them.

4. Plan your upcoming week in advance (sure there will be alterations, but plan nonetheless).

5. Practice self-discipline. It is okay to say no, especially to time sinks such as gossiping.

6. Seek the help of experts (advisers, friends, family, etc.) to lighten your load.

7. Avoid interruptions whenever possible (phone, e-mail).

8. Accomplish one task before beginning another.

9. Be organized, systematized.

10. Do unpleasant tasks first to "get them off your mind."

11. Understand when you perform different tasks best and build that into your schedule, if possible.

12. Use "waiting time" efficiently. Carry a book with you to read if you ride mass transit or listen to CDs in the car on subjects you want to learn.

Appendix C—Lifestyle Planning

The goal of this appendix is to help you determine and then achieve realistic, dynamic goals that create the lifestyle you want for yourself and your family. To begin, I would recommend the time-tested goal methodology, SMART. SMART is an acronym of the words Specific, Measurable, Attainable, Relevant, and Time-based. I would add a second acronym using the words Significant, Meaningful, Accountable, Realistic, and Thoughtful.

Specific—Clear definition of what you want to achieve

Measurable—Know when you have achieved your goal.

Attainable—You have the ability to achieve your goal; it is not impossible or even improbable.

Relevant—Something that makes you happy and motivated

Time-based—Deadline to help keep you on track

Significant—Something that can change your life and is worth pursuing with passion.

Meaningful—Something personal and worthy to you

Accountable—Knowing where you are in the process and that you are responsible for your actions

Realistic—Gets you out of your comfort zone but is within reach.

Thoughtful—Careful consideration of what makes you happy

Lifestyle planning begins with what I would call adequate management of your feelings and desires. Basically, it is creating an inventory of the positive feelings you would like to experience and then determining how you can reach them. You may also want to list those feelings you don't like and what happens to make you feel that way.

Secondly, determine why you are where you are. In other words, what motivated you to become the person you are today? Is it because of your parents, your spouse, your attitude, or something else?

Next, try to remember those times you made life-changing decisions. Why did those decisions have to be made at that particular time? What inputs did you factor into your decision-making process and was the result of the decision what you expected? Why or why not?

Since most people are trying to create a more balanced lifestyle, which areas need more attention? The major areas in your life include spiritual; health and wellness; financial; familial; and career. Rate each on a scale from one to ten.

Try to focus on the parts of your situation you are currently satisfied with. What did you do that resulted in the positive outcome? Can those actions become part of your actionable goal-setting and achievement process? How?

Since most people are not satisfied with everything in their lives, what parts leave you with an unsatisfied feeling? What did you do that resulted in the less-than-satisfying outcome? Why did you choose to do it that way?

Now that you have an idea of your past and present, we will try to create a future that transforms your dreams into reality. As I wrote in Chapter Two, Finding Your Balance, you have the ability to create your lifestyle, one day at a time. Think of your ideal day. What are you doing, who are you with, and how does that make you feel? Write it down and imagine being there. List the who, what, when, where, why, and how so you have an outline to work from. This outline provides the basis of your lifestyle plan.

Here is an example of a basic lifestyle plan that may help you create yours:

Title: My Life (shows ownership)

Who: Family, friends, and business relationships

Goal: Increase number of people I know and care about who have similar interests.

What: Being a successful husband, father, and wealth manager

Goal: Expand my business so I have the ability to be a blessing to more people and provide a better life for my family.

When: From this point forward

Goal: Double my business every five years. Spend two weeks per year on family vacations.

Where: Live during the summer and fall in Albuquerque, New Mexico. Live in southern Arizona, Florida, Hawaii, or southern California during the winter and spring (I am not fond of cold weather).

Goal: Purchase a second home by 2015 because I like to remain active year-round.

Why: I love what I do and want to help others create their own legacies.

How: Use my skills and abilities to help clients become and remain financially independent.

Now that you have a basic lifestyle plan, you have to be able to determine if they are SMART and how you will track your progress.

The following questions should help:

1. What do we dream about?

2. What is most important to us? (Your core values.)

3. Are we spending enough time with those we care about?

4. Are we having fun at work?

5. Do we enjoy our leisure time?

6. Where do we want to live?

7. What is the best way for us to maintain our health?

8. How much money do we need to retire?

9. Are we good community citizens?

10. What do we want our legacy to be?

Appendix D–
Risk Tolerance Questionnaire

Please answer the questions by circling one of the options. Choose the option that best indicates how you feel about each question. If none of the options is exactly right for you, choose the option that is closest. Please answer as honestly as possible.

This risk tolerance questionnaire is the property of FinaMetrica Pty Limited. Used by permission.

1. **Compared to others, how do you rate your willingness to take financial risks?**
   1. Extremely low risk taker
   2. Very low risk taker
   3. Low risk taker
   4. Average risk taker
   5. High risk taker
   6. Very high risk taker
   7. Extremely high risk taker

2. **How easily do you adapt when things go wrong financially?**
   1. Very uneasily
   2. Somewhat uneasily
   3. Somewhat easily
   4. Very easily

3. **When you think of the word "risk" in a financial context, which of the following words comes to mind first?**
   1. Danger
   2. Uncertainty
   3. Opportunity
   4. Thrill

4. **Have you ever invested a large sum in a risky investment mainly for the "thrill" of seeing whether it went up or down in value?**
   1. No
   2. Yes, very rarely
   3. Yes, somewhat rarely
   4. Yes, somewhat frequently
   5. Yes, very frequently

5. **If you had to choose between more job security with a small pay increase and less job security with a big pay increase, which would you pick?**
   1. Definitely more job security with a small pay increase
   2. Probably more job security with a small pay increase
   3. Not sure
   4. Probably less job security with a big pay increase
   5. Definitely less job security with a big pay increase

6. **When faced with a major financial decision, are you more concerned about the possible losses or the possible gains?**
   1. Always the possible losses
   2. Usually the possible losses
   3. Usually the possible gains
   4. Always the possible gains

7. **How do you usually feel about your major financial decisions after you make them?**
   1. Very pessimistic
   2. Somewhat pessimistic
   3. Somewhat optimistic
   4. Very optimistic

8. **Imagine you were in a job where you could choose to be paid salary, commission, or a mix of both. Which would you pick?**
   1. All salary
   2. Mainly salary
   3. Equal mix of salary and commission
   4. Mainly commission
   5. All commission

9. **What degree of risk have you taken with your financial decisions in the past?**
   1. Very small
   2. Small
   3. Medium
   4. Large
   5. Very large

10. **What degree of risk are you currently prepared to take with your financial decisions?**
    1. Very small
    2. Small
    3. Medium
    4. Large
    5. Very large

11. **Have you ever borrowed money to make an investment (other than for your home)?**
    1. No
    2. Yes

12. **How much confidence do you have in your ability to make good financial decisions?**
    1. None
    2. A little
    3. A reasonable amount
    4. A great deal
    5. Complete

13. **Suppose that five years ago you bought stock in a highly regarded company. That same year the company experienced a severe decline in sales due to poor management. The price of the stock dropped drastically and you sold at a substantial loss.**

    The company has been restructured under new management and most experts now expect it to produce better than average returns. Given your bad past experience with this company, would you buy stock now?
    1. Definitely not
    2. Probably not
    3. Not sure
    4. Probably
    5. Definitely

14. **Investments can go up and down in value and experts often say you should be prepared to weather a downturn. By how much could the total value of *all your investments* decrease before you would begin to feel uncomfortable?**
    1. Any fall in value would make me feel uncomfortable
    2. 10 percent
    3. 20 percent
    4. 33 percent
    5. 50 percent
    6. More than 50 percent

15. **Assume that a long-lost relative dies and leaves you a house in poor condition but is located in a suburb that's becoming popular.**

    As is, the house would probably sell for $300,000, but if you were to spend about $100,000 on renovations, the selling price would be around $600,000.

    However, there is some talk of constructing a major highway next to the house, and this would lower its value considerably.

    Which of the following options would you take?
    1. Sell it as is
    2. Keep it as is, but rent it out
    3. Take out a $100,000 mortgage and do the renovations

16. **Most investment portfolios have a mix of investments—some of the investments may have high expected returns but with high risk, some may have medium expected returns and medium risk, and some may be low-risk/low-return. (For example, stocks and real estate would be high-risk/high-return whereas cash and CDs would be low-risk/low-return.)**

    Which mix of investments do you find most appealing? Would you prefer all low-risk/low-return, all high-risk/high-return, or somewhere in between?

Please select one of the seven portfolios listed below.

Portfolio	Mix of Investment in Portfolio		
	High Risk/ Return	Medium Risk/ Return	Low Risk/ Return
1	0 percent	0 percent	100 percent
2	0 percent	30 percent	70 percent
3	10 percent	40 percent	50 percent
4	30 percent	40 percent	30 percent
5	50 percent	40 percent	10 percent
6	70 percent	30 percent	0 percent
7	100 percent	0 percent	0 percent

17. **You are considering placing one-quarter of your investment funds into a single investment. This investment is expected to earn about twice the CD rate. However, unlike a CD, this investment is not protected against loss of the money invested.**

    How low would the chance of a loss have to be for you to make the investment?
    1. Zero (no chance of loss_
    2. Very low chance of loss
    3. Moderately low chance of loss
    4. 50 percent chance of loss

18. **With some types of investment, such as cash and CDs, the value of the investment is fixed. However, inflation will cause the purchasing power of this value to decrease.**

    With other types of investment, such as stocks and real estate, the value is not fixed. It will vary. In the short term it may even fall below the purchase price. However, over the long term, the value of stocks and real estate should certainly increase by more than the rate of inflation.

With this in mind, which is more important to you, that the value of your investments does not fall or that it retains its purchasing power?

1. Much more important that the value does not fall
2. Somewhat more important that the value does not fall
3. Somewhat more important that the value retains its purchasing power
4. Much more important that the value retains its purchasing power

19. **In recent years, how have your personal investments changed?**
1. Always toward lower risk
2. Mostly toward lower risk
3. No changes or changes with no clear direction
4. Mostly toward higher risk
5. Always toward higher risk

20. **When making an investment, return and risk usually go hand-in-hand. Investments that produce above average returns are usually of above average risk.**

With this in mind, how much of the funds you have available to invest would you be willing to place in investments where both returns and risks are expected to be above average?
1. None
2. 10 percent
3. 20 percent
4. 30 percent
5. 40 percent
6. 50 percent
7. 60 percent
8. 70 percent
9. 80 percent
10. 90 percent
11. 100 percent

21. **Think of the average rate of return you would expect to earn on an investment portfolio over the next ten years. How does this compare with what you think you would earn if you invested the money in CDs?**
    1. About the same rate as from CDs
    2. About one and a half times the rate from CDs
    3. About twice the rate from CDs
    4. About two and a half times the rate from CDs
    5. About three times the rate from CDs
    6. More than three times the rate from CDs

22. **People often arrange their financial affairs to qualify for a government benefit or to obtain a tax advantage. However a change in legislation can leave them worse off than if they'd done nothing.**

    With this in mind, would you take a risk in arranging your affairs to qualify for a government benefit or obtain a tax advantage?
    1. I would not take a risk if there was any chance I could finish up worse off.
    2. I would take a risk if there was only a small chance I could finish up worse off.
    3. I would take a risk as long as there was more than a 50 percent chance that I would finish up better off.

23. **Imagine you are borrowing a large sum of money at some time in the future. It's not clear which way interest rates are going to move—they might go up, they might go down; no one seems to know. You could take a variable interest rate that will rise and fall as the market rate changes. Or you could take a fixed interest rate which is 1 percent more than the current variable rate but which won't change as the market rate changes. Or you could take a mix of both.**

How would you prefer your loan to be made up?

1. 100 percent variable
2. 75 percent variable, 25 percent fixed
3. 50 percent variable, 50 percent fixed
4. 25 percent variable, 75 percent fixed
5. 100 percent fixed

24. **Insurance can cover a wide variety of life's major risks—theft, fire, accident, illness, death, etc. How much coverage do you have?**
    1. Very little
    2. Some
    3. Considerable
    4. Complete

25. **This questionnaire is scored on a scale of 0 to 100. When the scores are graphed they follow the familiar bell-curve of the Normal distribution shown below. The average score is 50. Two-thirds of all scores are within 10 points of the average. Only 1 in 1000 is less than 20 or more than 80.**

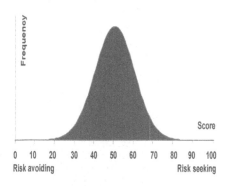

What do you think your score will be? _____

I hope this questionnaire increases your awareness of your attitudes, values, and experiences about finances. If you would like to see your score, and an analysis, please fax your questionnaire, with your contact information on a fax coversheet, to: 505-298-6656. This offer is limited to the first 100 who respond or by December 31, 2012, whichever occurs first.

This risk tolerance questionnaire is the property of FinaMetrica Pty Limited.
Used by Permission.

Appendix E—Questions to Ask an Estate Planning Attorney

Attorney Information

Name: _____

Business Name, if different: _____

Address: _____

City: _____ State: _____ Zip: _____

Phone:_____

About Your Practice

1. How many clients do you currently serve?
    ___ Fewer than 100   ___ 100–249   ___ 250-499   ___ 500+

2. What is your clients' most common estate planning concern> Please rank in order, with 1 being most common and 4 least common.

    1)_____   3) _____

    2)_____   4) _____

3. What is your clients' most common age range? Please rank in order on a scale from 1 to 4, with 1 being most common and 4 least common.

    ___ Under 35   ___ 36–50   ___ 51–65   ___ Over 65

4. What is your clients' most common net worth range? Please rank in order from 1 to 4 with 1 being most common and 4 least common.

___ < $1,000,000   ___ $1,000,001–$2,000,000

___ $2,000,001–$5,000,000   ___ > $5,000,000

5. Will you provide me with references from clients? ___ Yes ___ No

   a. Name: _____ Phone: _____

   b. Name: _____ Phone: _____

   c. Name: _____ Phone: _____

6. Will you provide me with a sample copy of a Will or Trust?

   ___ Yes ___ No

7. Do you have a succession plan? ___ Yes ___ No

   If yes, please provide a brief description here: _____

   _____

   _____

8. What is your company's mission statement? _____

   _____

   _____

Experience, Licenses, Education

9. How long have you been offering estate planning services? ___ yrs.

10. How long have you been licensed to practice law? ___ yrs.

11. What licenses (law, insurance, securities) and/or professional designations are you eligible to use?

    a. _____ / Yr. Received: _____

    b. _____ / Yr. Received: _____

    c. _____ / Yr. Received: _____

    d. _____ / Yr. Received: _____

    e. _____ / Yr. Received: _____

    f. _____ / Yr. Received: _____

12. What educational degrees have you earned?
   a. School: _____ Degree___ Major _____ Yr. ___
   b. School: _____ Degree___ Major _____ Yr. ___
   c. School: _____ Degree___ Major _____ Yr. ___

Services and Products

13. Which Estate Planning Services do you provide? Please check all that apply.
   ___ Last Will and Testament
   ___ Durable Power of Attorney for Health Care
   ___ Living Will
   ___ Durable Power of Attorney for Property
   ___ Living Trust
   ___ Alaska Trust
   ___ Dynasty Trust
   ___ Charitable Trusts
   ___ Family Limited Partnership
   ___ Guardianship
   ___ Conservatorship
   ___ Special Needs Trust
   ___ Probate
   ___ Business Continuation

14. Will you offer continuous advice?   ___ Yes   ___ No

15. Do you provide assistance with implementation?   ___ Yes ___ No

Compensation

16. How are you compensated? Please check all that apply.
   ___ Fee (specify):
       ___ Initial
       ___ Hourly
       ___ Retainer
   ___ Other (specify) _____

17. How is your compensation calculated? Please indicate all that apply.

    Based on an hourly rate of $ _____

    Fee range of $ _____ to $ _____

    Minimum fee of $ _____

    Other (specify)   _____

18. Are your fees negotiable? ___ Yes ___ No

19. Do you or any related party receive compensation from any persons or firms to whom I may be referred? ___ Yes ___ No

Regulatory and Compliance

If your answer to any of the following is "yes", please complete the section describing the event or proceeding. (Attach a separate explanation if necessary)

20. Has any court ever entered a judgment against you in connection with any legal advice activity? ___ Yes ___ No

21. Have you ever been involved in an arbitration proceeding that was settled or decided against you? ___ Yes ___ No

22. Have you ever been the subject of an order issued by a:

    a. Federal regulatory agency? ___ Yes ___ No

    b. State regulatory agency? ___ Yes ___ No

    c. Self-regulatory agency? ___ Yes ___ No

23. Have you been discharged or permitted to resign because you were accused of violating industry standards or legal practice related statutes? ___ Yes ___ No

24. Are you currently involved, directly, or indirectly, in any regulatory investigation or action, customer complaint, civil litigation, or criminal proceeding? ___ Yes ___ No
Description of event or proceeding:

_____

_____

_____

_____

_____

Appendix F—Family Budget Worksheet

Committed Expenses

Housing

    Mortgage (principal and interest) _____

    Real Estate Taxes _____

    Homeowners Insurance Premiums _____

    Rent Expense _____

    Electricity _____

    Gas (natural, fuel oil, propane, wood) _____

    Water, sewer, garbage _____

    Telephone _____

    Maintenance, repairs _____

Food (groceries) _____

Clothing

    Clothes _____

    Laundry, dry cleaning _____

Transportation

    Auto loan payment _____

    Auto insurance premium _____

Gasoline   _____
Auto maintenance, repairs   _____
Other (tolls, parking, license, registration)   _____

Health Care
Medical insurance premiums   _____
Medical care, prescriptions   _____
Dental insurance premiums   _____
Dental care   _____

Other Expenses
Life insurance premiums   _____
Disability insurance premiums   _____
Other insurance premiums (flood, umbrella)   _____
Education   _____
Dependent care (day care)   _____
Alimony payments   _____
Charge account payments   _____
Other loan payments   _____
Pet expenses   _____
Personal care (haircuts, cosmetics, etc.)   _____

Total Committed Expenses   _____

Discretionary Expenses

Entertainment, dining out, cable/satellite   _____
Communications (cell phone, Internet)   _____
Recreation (vacations, hobbies)   _____
Cash Charitable Contributions (tithes, offerings)   _____
Gifts   _____
Home Improvements (redecorating)   _____
Miscellaneous (books, downloads, subscriptions)   _____
Other (cigarettes, lessons, club dues, allowances)   _____

Total Discretionary Expenses _____

Savings and investments
Employee contributions to qualified retirement plans _____
Contributions to individual retirement accounts _____
Systematic investments _____
Total Savings and Investments _____

Tax Payments
Federal income tax (withholding, estimated payments _____
Social Security withholding (FICA) _____
State Income Tax (withholding, estimated payments) _____
Local Income Tax (withholding, estimated payments) _____
Total Tax Payments _____

Total Expenses _____

Income

Employment income, bonus _____
Self-employment income _____
Interest, dividends _____
Other income _____

Total Income _____

Discretionary Income (Income—Expenses) _____

Appendix G—Identifying Your Financial Values

Your financial plan should focus on the areas that are important to you and your family. This worksheet will help you list and prioritize your financial values *at this moment in your life*. Please use the scale of 1 being very important and 10 being not important.

1. Having money readily available for emergencies   ____

2. Having money readily available for opportunities   ____

3. Having financial protection against:
   a. Disability   ____
   b. Liability   ____
   c. Hospitalization   ____
   d. Premature Death   ____
   e. Long-Term Care   ____

4. Funding for education   ____

5. Gifting   ____

6. Charitable contributions   ____

7. Accumulating dollars for:
   a. Down payment on a home ____
   b. Vacation ____
   c. Car ____
   d. Other (Specify _____) ____

8. Minimizing income taxes ____

9. Minimizing estate taxes ____

10. Accumulating resources to provide retirement income ____

11. Estate planning ____

Reference Websites

United States Treasury: www.treasury.us.gov

Federal Reserve Board: www.federalreserve.gov

Social Security Administration: www.ssa.gov

Bureau of Labor Statistics: www.bls.gov

White House: www.whitehouse.gov

Investopedia: www.investopedia.com

Wikipedia: www.wikipedia.org

US Internal Revenue Service: www.irs.gov

Holy Bible: www.holybible.com or www.biblegateway.com

National Association of Insurance Commissioners: www.naic.org

Financial Industry Regulatory Authority: www.finra.org

Free Application for Federal Student Aid: www.fafsa.ed.gov

Affordable Care Act: www.healthcare.gov

Bibliography

Divorce Statistics: http://www.divorcestatistics.org. (n.d.)

Federal Reserve Board: http://www.federalreserve.gov. (n.d.)

Austin, D. A., and M. R. Levit (2011). *The Debt Limit: History and Recent Increases*. Washington, DC: Congressional Research Service.

Consumer Credit—G.19. (2012, February). Retrieved from Board of Governors of the Federal Reserve System: http://www.federalreserve.gov/releases/G19/Current/

"Facts for Consumers, Credit Repair—How to Help Yourself." Retrieved from www.ftc.gov/bcp/edu/pubs/consumer/credit/cre13.shtm. (n.d.)

Fisher, I. (1928). *The Money Illusion*. Martino Fine Books, Eastford, CT.

Freeman, A. L., and V. Srinivas (May 2011). "The next decade in global wealth among millionaire households." Retrieved from Deloitte Corporation website http://deloitte.com/us/globalwealth

Luntz, D. F. (2009). *What Americans Really Want … Really: Truth about Our Hopes, Dreams, and Fears*. New York, NY: Hyperion.

Self Storage Association. *Fact Sheet*. Retrieved from Self Storage Association http://www.selfstorage.org. (n.d.)

US Department of Labor, Bureau of Labor Statistics. (2011). *2010 American Time Use Survey*. Washington, DC: US Department of Labor.

Disclaimers

- The views expressed are of William E. Hauenstein, and should not be construed directly or indirectly as an offer to buy or sell any securities mentioned herein.

- All investing involves risk, including the potential loss of principal.

- There is no guarantee that a diversified portfolio will outperform a nondiversified portfolio in any given market environment.

- No investment strategy, including any referenced in this book, can guarantee a profit or protect against a loss in periods of declining values.

- Indexes cannot be invested in directly, are unmanaged, and do not incur management fees, costs, and expenses.

- Past performance is not a guarantee of future results.

- Information is based on sources to be reliable.

- This material does not in any way guarantee that our recommended investment approach is suitable for all investors.

- All examples are for illustration purposes only and are not intended to be a substitute for specific individualized tax, legal, investment, financial planning, or estate planning advice.

- As each individual situation is different, the information presented here should be relied upon only when coordinated with individual professional advice.

- In general, the bond market is volatile, as prices rise when interest rates fall and vice versa. This effect is usually pronounced for longer-term securities.

- Any fixed income security sold or redeemed prior to maturity may be subject to a substantial gain or loss.

- Sales of CDs prior to maturity may result in loss of principal and/or interest. Please discuss the amount of FDIC insurance available with your investment professional.

- A 529 plan is a college savings plan that allows individuals to save for college on a tax-advantaged basis. Every state offers at least one 529 plan. Before buying a 529 plan, you should enquire about the particular plan and its fees and expenses. You should also consider that certain states offer tax benefits and fee savings to in-state residents. Whether a state tax deduction and/or application fee savings are available depends on your state of residence. For tax advice, consult your tax professional. Nonqualifying distribution earnings may be subjected to taxes and penalties.

- Savings bonds, including Series EE bonds, must be held at least one year before they can be redeemed. If they are held for fewer than five years, a penalty of three months' interest will be assessed when the bonds are redeemed. Interest from savings bonds is tax-deferred while you own the bonds, but those taxes come due when you sell.

- The risks in mutual funds vary depending upon the strategy used by the fund as well as the sectors in which the fund invests. When redeemed, shares may be worth more or less than the original amount invested.

Index

148

health wellness plan, 73–74
health-care directives, 82
heritage planning, 93
Holy Bible, 139
home equity line of credit, 39
homeowner's insurance, 24, 43
hourly fee planners/advisers, 92
housing bubble, 21
housing expenses, way to reduce in
    retirement, 64–65

I

I bonds, 54, 56, 94, 144
impulse buying (in US), 9
individual equities, 34, 94. *See also*
    equities
individual fixed income securities, 33–34
INF (Intermediate-Range Nuclear
    Forces) Treaty, 4
inflation, 61–62, 74
inflation risk, 34
information, compared to advice, 100
inheritance, 83
inherited IRA, 85
innate ability, identification of, 7–8
inputs of complex situations, importance
    of analyzing, 3–4
insurance
    about, 42–43
    analysis of needs, 83
    as aspect of financial planning, 93
    auto insurance, 43
    as basic, 26
    casualty insurance, 43–45
    and commission-based advisers, 93
    disability insurance, 46–49
    health insurance, 23–24, 27, 46–47
    homeowner's insurance, 24, 43
    liability insurance, 24, 43
    life insurance, 24, 45–46
    long-term care insurance, 26, 71, 75
    property insurance, 43–45
    self-insurance, 74
    state insurance plans, for uninsurable,
        47
    temporary health insurance, 27

term life insurance, 24
insurance agent, 100
interest rate risk, 32, 34
Intermediate-Range Nuclear Forces
    (INF) Treaty, 4
international phone calls, 67
Internet
    blogs and chat sessions for support,
        75
    "free land," 65
    information on mutual funds, 31
    senior discounts, 66
    websites. *See* websites
investment adviser, 57, 60, 68, 80, 91,
    94, 99–100
investment management, 93
investment portfolios, 36
investment risk, 31, 33–34
Investopedia, 139
investors, becoming savers, 4
IRAs
    beneficiary designations for, 82
    college savings plan as similar to, 54
    education IRAs, 54
    inheritance of, 84–89
    inherited IRA, 85
    as intangible financial asset, 80
    investments inside of, as compared to
        ESAs, 55
    as option in defined contribution
        plan, 59
    Roth IRAs, 86–89
    traditional IRAs, 84–87
issuer risk (unsystematic risk), 34

J

jobs, projected as fastest growing, 28
3 John 1:2, 74

K

Keynes, John Maynard, 13
knowledge, as power, 3